For Fr... P9-AFD-656

May you follow
in your mothers
footsteps
AND take the
pleasure world one
level further!

love James

The Discipline of Pleasure

JAMES BAMPFIELD

LANNOO CAMPUS

D/2014/45/9 | ISBN 978 94 014 1288 9 | NUR 740

COVER DESIGN   Studio Derycke
BOOK DESIGN   LetterLust | Stefaan Verboven

LannooCampus Publishers is a subsidiary of
Lannoo Publishers, the book and multimediadivision
of Lannoo Publishers nv.

Uitgeverij LannooCampus
Erasme Ruelensvest 179 bus 101 | 3001 Leuven | Belgium

www.lannoocampus.be

To my son, Sidney, prince of pleasure

Contents

Introduction

I HAVE HAD TWO TYPES OF SCHOOLING IN MY LIFE: WHAT I call an old schooling and a new schooling. My old schooling was traditional, English-style boarding school: typical upper-middle class, nudged and thumped through the ranks of private school and privilege. I was a good fit in the sense that I was competent in class and on the sports field. Privilege does not always pamper, however, and it was a rough ride. Some of it I loved, some of it continued to give me nightmares into my later years, as fear was the dominant motivator at such a school.

What did I learn?

I learnt that duty comes first, that doing the right thing comes first.

I learnt to win. I acquired a steely resolve, which did its best to keep in check a lurking, tenacious undertow of emotion and insecurity that rarely left me.

Pleasure was driven underground, into illicit escapades and rendezvous. Study was a means to an end and enjoyment came from doing well, not from learning itself. There were occasional Dead Poet Society-type teachers who would inject a dose of colour and joy into the classroom, but the general ethos was one of grinding out results... which I duly did.

It is remarkable how little memory I have of being told to *enjoy* a game while playing sport. I was representing the school and the maxim we heard *ad nauseam* was: do your best and fight to the end! Perseverance was the most praised quality.

Looking back, it is easy to despise and mock this kind of schooling, but that is not how I feel. Although some of it was tragic and some of it was comical, there was a basic orientation towards what I now call *soul pleasure*. I feel sad, however, because this basic orientation was poorly articulated and even more poorly applied. No one learnt how to be happy.

At the core of the British psyche is an aridity, an essential lack of juice – of joy! – which has plagued me all my life. *Love* is the chief ingredient of pleasure and love is the one thing we never learnt, neither giving nor receiving. That is why the greatest British 'achievement', the Empire, is its most flawed. Head and gut, but no heart… and everyone has suffered the consequences.

I too have a good head on my shoulders and a drive from my belly, which have brought me much, but my heart needs both constant reassurance and provocation to unlock its capacity for feeling and joy.

My second schooling came in the form of spirituality.

From the age of 16, I plunged headlong into a world of gurus, therapy and spiritual practice that was in great contrast (and occasional similarity) to boarding school life. It was common for me to move from the gowns of Trinity College to the meditation robes of Satsang, from the cries of the football pitch to the cries of the primal therapy room.

The new schooling was also a tough ride. Young and brittle, I was easily bruised by the rigour of therapeutic 'encounter' and numbed to the knees by the discipline of meditation. That said, I was also introduced to the wonders of the world of spirit and a whole new dimension of life opened up to me in all its splendour.

I wouldn't give up those roller-coaster years for anything; travelling from country to country, community to community, teacher to teacher, teaching to teaching. I was on the road to enlightenment and nothing could stand in my way. Except myself.

I slowly got more and more in my own way. Thank God.

There came a point when I realized, almost as an afterthought, that I wasn't happy. At that moment, my quest for truth lost its lustre.

I always felt – still do – that some ultimate state of contentment is possible, that the veil of separation could disappear once and for all, revealing a glorious unity. I wasn't experiencing this in any continuous way though and I was suffering.

'Truth' is a masculine kind of goal and in a strange way retains echoes of my British upbringing. I was tired of the sweat and effort. I was tired of the tension of the trail and the constant pushing of boundaries. I didn't want to 'boldly go' any more.

I longed for a softer, more pleasure-oriented approach to life. I needed to come home. To myself.

And I don't mean to some higher self, some universal self. Just to James. The path of learning and development needed to be anchored more in my actual inner state, more in my body, more in my own wisdom.

I had been told during all those years that happiness is not the goal of the true spiritual seeker. Most Eastern religions suggest that any form of duality – such as pleasure and pain – is beside the point. I decided, however, that the pursuit of truth (in any form) was an incomplete truth at best, especially if that truth had been decreed outside myself. It was time to kill the Buddha and reclaim my own sense of knowing.

Neither of my schools taught me how to enjoy life. Implicitly or explicitly, both schools were suspicious of pleasure.

I have no doubt that my spiritual education has contributed enormously to my wellbeing, and indeed this book, but there remains a hole, which I am here trying to fill.

I continue to draw inspiration from truth-oriented practices, but the edges have been softened and I no longer see truth as an end-goal. What use is truth if it doesn't improve the *felt* quality of life?

When I look around me, I see people crying out for liberation and joy, not truth. I see a world that has for too long prized truth ahead of pleasure – and even pain ahead of pleasure. Pain is still revered and the crosses we choose to bear are given great respect. People go on hunger strikes, not binge strikes. Our myths tend to glorify hardship as heroism above all else.

I am, like many others, so very tired of what I call the 'truth wars': endless cycles of violence, sometimes on a huge scale, perpetrated mostly by men who wish to impose their version of truth on others. I also know that placing a rigid moral straightjacket on the perpetrators simply perpetuates the truth war. I long for a society that gives more attention to simple and spiritual pleasures than to the ego pleasures of power, domination and revenge. I long to ask those in power what *really* makes them happy, what *really* gives them pleasure...

I have been living in Belgium for the past 12 years and I experience here a more subtle kind of oppression... people trying so hard to do the right thing: be a good worker, be a good father, be a good wife. Such a keen sense of duty and responsibility elevates the Belgians above a certain self-indulgence that I have experienced in other cultures, but also weighs them down with a dense energy of resignation. Life is rarely celebrated other than in specifically designated contexts. People are taught to build and sweat, but not to fly and delight.

So perhaps it is not surprising that my paean to pleasure was born in Belgium, though it feels like my whole life experience is poured into this book.

In my job as consultant and facilitator, I have worked with thousands of people and seen a more or less universal longing for a greater quality of life and deeper fulfilment. Unfortunately, you either have people who feel ashamed or guilty about focusing on their own pleasure, deeming it selfish or immoral, or you have those who focus on pleasure in a superficial way and have no awareness or discipline to help them find the deeper pleasures in life.

Clearly I am not the only one moving away from a truth and duty-oriented life. Happiness is in fashion these days and fast becoming an important measuring stick, individually and even politically. I welcome this movement.

I also distance myself slightly from the happiness movement though, and purposely choose the word *pleasure* because it is a more fundamental part of our make-up (children are not concerned with happiness) and because the pleasure mechanics are less prone to self-delusion and outside influence. We can kid ourselves that we are happy, but it is harder to kid ourselves that we are experiencing pleasure.

As I will explain, happiness is just a sophisticated form of pleasure that includes a sense of duration.

The way I write is the way I have lived: eclectic, impressionistic and without much sense of order. I quote philosophers and spiritual pundits in a fairly reckless manner that will offend some and attract others. I have philosophical leanings but am not a philosopher. I have spiritual leanings but am neither disciple nor guru. Just a fellow traveller who might have visited more or different countries than you.

I have taken great pains and re-writes to find the right balance between head and heart though it could well be that the final integration of the two awaits a further breakthrough in my personal evolution. The first draft of the book clearly suffered from delusions of intellectual grandeur and I received signals from pilot readers that their pleasure levels were strikingly low. I must say that on various occasions while reading the (many) philosophical treatises on pleasure, I have also at times felt like I was losing the will to live... One general principle I have deduced so far that guides existing philosophical, sociological and scientific writers on pleasure is: give the reader as little pleasure as possible.

My hope is to inspire and light a flame of pleasure in your heart. There are no tools, no workbooks, just a bunch of reflections, musings and insights. You, and only you, can do the rest...

What is Pleasure?

Pleasure is the gentle spray of sunrays on my wintery skin, slowly seeping down into stiff bones. Pleasure is the rustle of autumn leaves between my feet. Pleasure is my first kiss, birds singing in my wild heart. Pleasure is the feel of my child's head nestled between shoulder and chest as I carry him to bed in a bubble of love and trust. Pleasure is stroking my dog, pleasure is hearing my wife laugh unashamedly, pleasure is feeling the champagne bubbles explode gently on my tongue.

Pleasure is fixing a broken tap, pleasure is solving a crossword puzzle, pleasure is winning a Nintendo game (apparently). Pleasure is skiing recklessly down the mountainside at full speed, relishing the bite of wind and risk on my cheeks. Pleasure is lunging to hit a perfect tennis volley. Pleasure is looking at my shiny car after I have scrubbed away. Pleasure is teaching my son how to read a clock, pleasure is serving my family as best I can. Pleasure is helping an elderly person with her bags. Pleasure is creating a work of art. Pleasure is getting results, doing a good job. Pleasure is fulfilling my mission, enacting my values, helping to make a better world.

Pleasure is meeting you for real. Pleasure is intimacy – sharing, exposing, disclosing. Heaven is other people. Pleasure is meeting you, the other. Seeing and being seen. Pleasure is comradeship and trust. Pleasure is being part of a band of brothers and sisters, the team, the gang. Pleasure is feeling you beside me, my wife and partner, as we face the world together.

Pleasure is passion, pleasure is penetration, pleasure is caressing, pleasure is making love. Pleasure is love.

Pleasure is seeing the Taj Mahal and rubbing my eyes in disbelief at such grace. Pleasure is hearing that one melody that pierces my defences and confronts me with a beauty so fierce as to leave my tiny whining self in pieces. Pleasure is being confounded and transported by a painting, which plunges me into new waters.

Pleasure is when I finally sink out of my thinking mind into a sweet presence of being that knows and needs no desire or goal. Pleasure is when all becomes transparent, no veil, no separation: pleasure is when 'I' am gone. The movie of my life goes on but something extraordinary has happened to the part of me watching it... what was an I is now vast, empty and tainted with bliss.

Sounds pretty good, doesn't it? Life offers an endless array of joys and pleasures, some readily available, some elusive, some buried, some yet to be discovered. The word 'abundance' doesn't do justice to the diverse and sumptuous catalogue of pleasure dangled before us in this slice of life we are given.

But before we celebrate too wildly, here is another take on pleasure:

Pleasure is revenge. Pleasure is humiliating my wife when she has humiliated me. Pleasure is cutting someone down with the sword of my tongue. Pleasure is turning the whip on myself when I am already desperate. Pleasure is injecting myself with heroin. Pleasure is lashing out at others when my own pain is too much to bear.

Atrocities can even bear the stamp of pleasure for some.

If such diverse recipes of experience all contain the ingredient of pleasure, how is pleasure best understood? Foucault says nobody knows what pleasure really is. Freud says pleasure and displeasure are "the darkest and most impenetrable area of the psyche".

Yet every child, every adult, can directly report on any given experience in terms of pleasure and displeasure. Even when the two are entwined, they can both be named, distinguished, with confidence. Pleasure is a fundamental element of our internal world – immediately recognizable. We are continuously registering and responding to pleasure (and its opposites).

How can something so simple, so basic, be so mysterious? We can talk of neurotransmitters or the release of dopamine in the bloodstream but these are just the physical, biological correlates of the experience – such facts don't help us understand and interpret the *felt texture* of the experience.

In his book *Happiness*, the Dalai Lama – as many others have before him – makes a distinction between pleasure and happiness. I see no fundamental difference; we are still talking about *what feels good*. Happiness is just a sophisticated form of pleasure that includes the concept of duration: a subtle form of pleasure drawn out over time. Our first experience as children is of pleasure, not happiness, as we have little concept of time. Pleasure is the basic experience and drive out of which adult forms such as happiness and contentment can grow.

If the line we draw to distinguish between pleasure and happiness is too thick, we run the risk of dishonoring the roots of happiness and forgetting that the quest for pleasure and happiness stem from the same impulse. People would like to think, for example, that the desire for chocolate and the quest for moral or spiritual contentment are different. The pleasure impulse fuels both equally. All we ever want is what feels good.

So let us return to the simple definition and leave the rest in mystery: pleasure is that which pleases us. This book is more about our puzzling *relationship* to pleasure than the puzzle of pleasure itself.

I am advocating in the course of this book a new kind of hedonism. Through my *typology of pleasure*, I will lay out what I believe to be a new map of pleasure and explain the discipline and personal developmental process needed to apply this map. I believe my brand of neo-hedonism can help make the world a happier place for all.

In the course of this pleasure treatise I wish to dispel certain misconceptions about pleasure. When I first started announcing to friends and colleagues the theme of my book, there was much suspicion about the word pleasure and encouragement to change it. That very suspicion is one of the reasons why I think the book needs to be written.

I like the word pleasure because its sensual flavour brings us back down to the earth of our bodies. Pleasure takes us out of pretense; it releases us from the pinching grip of our lofty notions as to what *should* be good for us and others. Pleasure brings a lush humility.

Psychologist Carol Gilligan expresses a similar notion in her wonderful book, *The Birth of Pleasure*:

"The English word pleasure is a sensual word, the z of the 's' and the sound of the 'u' coming from deep within our bodies, tapping the wellsprings of desire and curiosity, a knowing that resides within ourselves."

Pleasure is that which pleases. Happiness, joy, satisfaction, contentment, bliss, cheerfulness, rapture, ecstasy, fulfilment, merriment, delight, gladness, glee, gratification, relish, delectation... these are all different colours of the pleasure spectrum. These emotions and states may differ in degree and duration, but they all bear the unmistakable stamp of pleasure: they please us.

In order to bring credibility and dignity to the word and pursuit of pleasure, I will try to relieve pleasure of various associated misconceptions that have gathered over the years:

1   A life devoted to pleasure means *dissipation* and *excess*. The reason pleasure is so often associated with excess is because it is on the one hand judged, minimalized and repressed, and on the other hand secretly glorified, longed for and worshipped. The *discipline* of pleasure does not lead to an excess of anything. A hedonism infused with *learning* does not lead to decadence.

2   Pleasure is synonymous with *fun*. During the Haiti earthquake disaster in 2010, there was a heart-rending radio interview with a foreign doctor who had flown out to help and had been working 24/7 to treat a horrific array of injuries. At one point he was asked how it felt to be doing what he was doing. There was a silence and eventually he answered in a voice cracked with emotion: "It is as awful as you would imagine... and there is nowhere else in the world I want to be." I realized in that moment how much *pleasure* this man was deriving from playing his part in the crisis. It would be inaccurate (and inappropriate) to imagine he was having *fun* in that context, but the fact that it *pleased* and *satisfied* him to be there cannot be denied. Furthermore, on hearing his words I was deeply touched and felt the pleasure of being touched.

3 Pleasure refers only to *nice* experiences. Too often, pleasure has sweet, superficial associations. I once had a painful swollen toe, which only seemed to get worse. I couldn't work out what the problem was, so I eventually consulted a doctor friend, who proceeded to draw out a huge, bloody splinter, which had been submerged in my toe for several months. The experience was deeply satisfying if painful. Could this be described as a *nice* experience?

Similarly, can an emotional meltdown – tears of pain and relief – be described as a *nice* experience? Perhaps this is why Freud tended to define pleasure as a release of tension – and therefore orgasm as the greatest pleasure. I don't think pleasure can be restricted to the release of tension, but I do think that covers a large domain of pleasure.

4 Pleasure presupposes *immorality*. This is the most common challenge to pleasure, as I shall explore in chapter 3. How can pleasure be 'good' if revenge and spite (and much worse) can bring pleasure? This is why Plato calls pleasure the "bait of evil", as do many other sages in as many words. Pleasure is often pitted against virtue and moral goodness. One of the aims of this book is to place morality *within* the pleasure spectrum, not in opposition to it.

5 The pursuit of pleasure or hedonism is inherently *unspiritual*. In the philosophical world, hedonists have tended to be atheist. In common usage, a weekend devoted to pleasure is not readily associated with church or a meditation retreat. *Spirit pleasure*, however, provides a whole category in my pleasure typology. I will show that not only does the transpersonal domain offer some of the most profound pleasures, but also that the discipline of pleasure eventually *leads* us to spirituality.

The reason I take pleasure so seriously is because it is an *end in itself*. An end state, an end value. Try playing this game and see if you can get further than pleasure (or a definition of pleasure) as your motivation:

Why do you play sport?
Because I like moving my body.
Why do you like moving your body?
Because it feels good.
Why do you like something that feels good?
Um… strange question!

Or:
Why do you like playing sport?
Because I like competing.
Why do you like competing?
To prove something.
Why do you like proving something?
Because then I feel powerful.
Why do you like feeling powerful?
Because it feels good.
Why do you like something that feels good?
Um…

My definition of pleasure is broad and includes everything that feels good. I wish to strip the word of certain assumptions and restore some of its innocence, while honouring its status as the only true end goal. Broad as the ocean, pleasure also has the variations of both depth and menace, from sparkling shallows to deep blue chasms, from silky calm to vicious currents.

I like the way David Constantine elucidates on the subject in this poem:

Pleasure

A poem, like the clitoris, is there
For pleasure and although some experts say
It can't be only pleasure it is there for
But must do something else to pay its way
But what that something else is can't agree
We leave them to their wrangling and say
The pleasure principle will do for you and me.

The Pleasure Impulse

"Nature has placed mankind under the government of two sovereign masters, pain and pleasure."
– Jeremy Bentham

I WATCH MY YOUNG SON WHO, LIKE ALL KIDS I HAVE MET, seems to live for pleasure. Though his discipline is questionable, he has the drive to become an expert hedonist. His endless appetite for pleasure, indeed his utter commitment to the cause of pleasure, never ceases to astonish me. Be it a toy, a game, a cuddle, a sweet, a song – he will drain every last drop of pleasure from the day.

We once took him on a trip through the Sinai desert with a few other families. Camped with the Bedouin: no electricity, no gadgets, no toilets… just sand, sun and stars. This band of kids, who didn't know each other before they landed in the desert together, managed to entertain themselves royally from the first day to the last. In pursuit of their pleasure goal, they showed an imagination, devotion and proactivity that would have won an adult an entrepreneur-of-the-year award.

Love of pleasure exists from the start.

As does the other side of the coin: the avoidance of pain.

This two-sided impulse seems fundamental, as if linked to our very life force.

So where does this appetite for pleasure go as we get older?

The answer is nowhere. We are born wanting pleasure and avoiding pain, and we die wanting pleasure and avoiding pain. From the moment we wake up in the morning, we make countless choices based on the pleasure/pain compass.

Which cereal shall I eat today? Actually, maybe I will go wild and opt for an egg! Why? Anticipated pleasure.

Or I will go without breakfast because I've been putting on weight. Why? Anticipated pain of shame.

Or, being a creature of habit, I will have my usual cornflakes and coffee. Why? The familiarity makes me feel comfortable – change can be unpleasant and disturbing.

Now I am at the office, shall I answer the difficult email first or the easy ones? Shall I defer the pleasure or the pain?

As the day develops, I begin to ask questions about my job.

Is it right for me? Does it make me happy? Does it bring me pleasure? Well, it does bring me plenty of money, which I also associate with pleasure and happiness… but does it fulfil me? Does it challenge me? Do I look forward to going to work? Is my work meaningful?

These are all pleasure-oriented questions. Happiness, after all, is just an adult form of pleasure.

At lunchtime I am presented with a dilemma. *Do I go on a lunch date with a former girlfriend I found on Facebook? I haven't yet told my wife that we've been in touch… I anticipate the thrill of meeting the ex again after all these years, but I also anticipate the discomfort of withholding (what might be considered) important information from my wife. Or worse still, she might find out and give me hell! On second thoughts, it is unlikely that she will find out. But I have an ideal in my mind of an open relationship in which we tell each other everything. Breaking that would be painful.*

All our thoughts, feelings and actions are in some way connected to the pleasure impulse. I am not saying everything can be *reduced* to the pleasure impulse, but it is omnipresent, either lurking in the background or thrusting itself into the foreground.

As I will explain in more depth in later chapters, moral questions too are connected to pleasure and pain. Consider the expression: "I couldn't live with myself [if I lied to her...]" The implication of this example is that living with a lie is painful and therefore to be avoided. What if our greatest motivation is to avoid hurting others (for example, if she discovers the lie)? The pain of others is only meaningful because we empathize and share the pain of others. In other words, the pain of others *also hurts us.*

Is it mean and selfish to care about the suffering of others only because it causes us pain too? On the contrary! It is that very empathy that makes us human. If we didn't suffer to some extent *with* others, how could we feel compassion?

The pleasure impulse infiltrates our every act and attitude.

While I was writing this book, an old friend, someone I deeply loved and respected, someone who was helping me with this project, killed himself. The horror of his death still makes me shudder, moistens my eyes. Again and again I have asked myself what could have brought him to this act of violence. The only conclusion I can come to is that the pain of dying was less to him than that of living. He was avoiding (anticipated) suffering.

To take the rather extreme and painful example of suicide further, studies of suicide letters suggest there is often some intended pleasure from the communication in the letter, be it the tiniest morsel of comfort in imagining how they will be missed, or how others will finally share in their suffering – a kind of revenge.

If the pleasure impulse is fundamental to being human – and animal? – we can infer that the pleasure impulse is more nature than nurture. In Freudian terms, the impulse is *id* versus *superego*, instinctive rather than conditioned.

The external source of pleasure may vary as we grow older according to culture and social context, but the apparatus itself would appear to be a universal given from the word go. Milk and warmth: pleasure. Cold and hunger: pain.

As an infant gets older and a 'self' begins to form, registering pleasure and pain turns into *willing* pleasure. A strategic attitude towards pleasure and pain develops that will eventually result in the sorts of complex deliberations of my day at work as described above.

Psychoanalysts will argue that much of the pleasure/pain apparatus remains submerged in the unconscious and from there influences our attitudes and behaviour. That may well be so, but this fact only reinforces the omnipresence of the pleasure impulse, as it is seen to inform both our conscious and subconscious minds. In fact, part of the *discipline* of pleasure – the learning process connected to the kinds of pleasure I am advocating – will involve uncovering some of those subconscious forces at work and liberating us from their sabotage of our pleasure.

Congruent with the Judaeo-Christian culture in which I have grown up, I have spent a large part of my life struggling against the pleasure impulse, trying to conquer it, trying to manipulate it.

As Plato says, pleasure is the "bait of evil". Pleasures are "guilty". Pleasures are "wicked". The moral hammer is easily raised when the word pleasure arises. Pursuit of pleasure is often seen as a vice, represented by illicit sex, illicit drugs, dissipation and decadence.

Yet the demonization of the pleasure impulse contains a fundamental contradiction: Why would we want to conquer the pleasure demons other than to have greater pleasure or greater happiness?

I don't believe we can defeat or transcend entirely the pleasure impulse – not while we still have a body or physical form, not while we are still human. Even transcendence is a means to a deeper level of pleasure. We need to accept and honour the pleasure impulse – guide it, refine it, even transform it, but as a friend, not an enemy.

Treat the pleasure impulse as an enemy and it will have its revenge. Suppress the pleasure impulse to the cellar of your psyche and it will creep back up through the cracks in the walls like rising damp. Why do you think the monk whips himself in contrition for his sinful pleasures of the flesh? Because the pain gives him some kind of pleasure, some kind of release. Ban the wares of the pleasure vendor and they will simply go underground and reappear on the black market.

I see the pleasure impulse as God's great gift to us. Without it, what is our *raison d'être*? Without it, why would we seek a happier life? Without anticipated increase in pleasure and decrease in pain, why would we try to create a good life for ourselves? The pleasure impulse is the seed of our own evolution: as individuals, as societies, as a planet. Through seeking deeper and deeper levels of pleasure we can become freer and wiser.

Yes, not *more* pleasure, but *deeper* pleasure. Seeking only quantity of pleasure can lead us astray, even imprison us. True hedonism seeks quality, not quantity, of pleasure; the true hedonist is like a surfer looking for the perfect wave. This takes discipline and learning. And *un*learning: peeling away the psychological and cultural obstructions to pleasure. The pleasure impulse is in some ways blind and brute, unrefined.

As Freud points puts, when we grow older the 'pleasure principle' bumps up against the 'reality principle', and we have to learn how to juggle the two in order to get the best pleasure out of life. As we mature, we realize that our environment is not merely an extension of us (as in the mind of the infant) but has its own separate reality, which may or may not be able to meet our needs and desires. Out of this realization eventually comes the concept of 'deferred gratification', as we learn that in order to gain certain pleasures we may first have to do something else that is not quite so pleasurable. For example, we first have to be sweet to Mama in order to receive a sweetie.

Of course there are many other views as to what constitute the fundamental human drives. Evolutionary psychologists will point to survival and genetic reproduction. Freud – who lost faith in the 'dominion' of the pleasure principle because he felt it couldn't account for the astonishing amount of self-destructive behaviour he witnessed in his patients, and society as whole – came up with another drive, the 'death instinct', that seeks a return to the inorganic and inanimate state from which we came and will ultimately return.

Some look at fundamental human drives from a totally different angle: they say that there are external factors behind our behaviour that are as strong as, or even stronger than the internal drives: karma, God, the Devil, destiny, or any other mysterious cosmic force.

I believe in all of the above to a certain extent, apart possibly from the Devil (and I may of course pay a gruesome price for such naivety). These other drives are not incompatible with the pleasure

THE DISCIPLINE OF PLEASURE

impulse. I am not convinced, for example, that the death instinct is divorced from the pleasure principle. On the one hand, death, as an image of pain, is to be avoided; on the other hand death can also be seen symbolically – and even literally in the case of suicide – as deliverance from pain. Destruction can bring us to rest…

As for external drives such as karma, the wheel of life and so on, yes maybe but the pleasure impulse sits more securely within our circle of influence than a visit to the three Fates bent over their wheel, spinning our destinies.

No matter their philosophical leaning, everyone can attest at least to the existence of the pleasure impulse. The impulse is a given and we can use it. The pleasure impulse offers an immediate, universally recognizable, and practical tool for life.

But surely, you might say, we are using this tool all the time anyway? Yes, we are, but not effectively. Most of us do not connect pleasure to discipline, to learning. We do not reflect deeply enough on what gives us the greatest pleasure.

When I look back at my life I see that I have at times gone to astonishing lengths of self-deception and denial when facing the simple question: am I happy? Am I enjoying life? Often we ignore the question altogether, grit our teeth and undergo the torments we assume to be our inescapable lot.

We rarely ask these questions out of sincere inquiry. They are scary questions: the answer might lead to change, internal or external. We might have to end a relationship or job; we might have to admit that we have nothing of substance to complain about. We might have to explore what stops us from enjoying what is on our plate. We might also have to admit that we often sabotage deep experience of pleasure by opting for poor quality pleasure.

For example, let's take a look at the topical 'junk flow'. The average person in an economically developed society will reportedly spend at least 10 years of their life in front of a screen. Ten years! We choose to glue ourselves to the screen because it brings us *some* pleasure. Most of the time junk flow doesn't bring a lot of pleasure, but it does register, albeit faintly, on what the poet Keats called the 'pleasure thermometer'.

Pleasure comes largely as a result of our absorption in the junk flow. Like a child with a toy, we like to be immersed in an activity that takes all our attention and feels like a seamless flow between us and our environment. Famous (in spite of his unpronounceable name) psychologist Csikszentmihalyi has researched this topic and persuasively links 'flow' to pleasure, joy and even rapture. Out of his work have arisen expressions such as 'in the zone'. Junk flow is simply the most readily available form of flow: it brings instant immersion.

When I come away from a junk flow session at the laptop, I usually feel dull and without energy, even grumpy. When I come out of a deeper flow – a tennis match, a music concert, a challenging seminar with a client, a profound and touching conversation with someone, even, sometimes, writing – I feel vital and energized. My eyes look out on a sparkling world. This is *optimal flow*.

But how often do I choose the junk flow despite knowing I could do better? Of course junk flow serves a purpose in our lives, and may even protect us from certain painful truths, but for most people most of the time it is an automatic, pleasure-limiting habit.

To be clear, I am not judging junk flow from an ethical perspective: "It simply isn't good for you, dear!" I am judging it from a pleasure perspective: does it make us happy? Junk flow may bring pleasure, but of what depth?

Our comparison of junk flow and optimal flow is a comfortable one. A less comfortable one would be a comparison between, say, volunteer work in Africa and an act of cruelty. Both these activities involve the pleasure impulse in some way. Apart from other, subconscious factors, the volunteer is seeking satisfaction by being generous and helping alleviate the suffering of others, fulfilling a mission, or feeling morally upright.

The perpetrator of cruelty is seeking satisfaction through a sense of power, or perhaps through revenge, or setting things straight, or the comfort of serving and belonging to a group identity that approves this particular act of cruelty. Don't kid yourself: we all commit cruelties, both in thought and action – and part of our motivation is pleasure.

As mentioned earlier, the pleasure impulse is blind and brute. The impulse itself neither discerns nor measures. This is where *discipline* comes in.

My analysis above is based on pleasure criteria, not on ethical grounds. That is exactly the perspective shift I am trying to bring.

As we will see shortly, the pleasure perspective is perhaps a more effective means of reducing evil than an ethical perspective.

To summarize, I am making two points about the pleasure impulse:
1 The pleasure impulse is an omnipresent given that needs to be embraced.
2 The movement towards deeper, greater pleasure requires discipline and learning – as will be further explored in the chapter 'Soul Pleasure'.

Problems with Pleasure

"Pleasure blinds the eyes of the mind and has no fellowship with virtue."
  – Cicero

So what to do with this blind and brute drive for pleasure?

Over the years I would say that society has come up with various general categories of response to the pleasure impulse. Let me introduce you to a few fictitious characters who embody these categories. Although we will naturally gravitate towards one category, to a certain extent all these characters exist in us.

Meet Moralist Mark, named after Roman senator Marcus Tullius, quoted above.

> *Moralist Mark lives in all of us to different degrees.*
> *I feel him whispering sharply in my ear,*
> *judgments from on high,*
> *splitting, polarizing, doubting.*
> *Vague but persistent echoes of guilt,*
> *acid showers of should's and shouldn't's,*
> *fears of being caught out, fears of punishment,*
> *images of church, images of parents, images of school teachers*
> *flitting like ghoulish moths through my mind.*

Somewhere, somehow, pleasure is bad.
Pleasure goes back to the forbidden fruit,
the luscious apple we were never meant to taste.
I feel Moralist Mark and his religious successors always pushing me up:
up to 'better' things, up out of the swamp of desire.
Disdain and transcend these earthly pleasures!
This ascendant path of the moralist severs us from our bodies,
mocks and denigrates sensual pleasures,
disassociates us from our roots, uglifies planet earth,
denigrates the feminine.

The ascendant path can lead to great pleasures – pleasures of the soul, pleasures of the spirit – but too often it is fuelled by fear of what lies below. Fear of matter, fear of body, fear of sensuality, fear above all of SEX. This fear will diminish the ascendent joys above and cause havoc and destruction in the world of the flesh below Witches will be burnt, adulterers will be stoned, sinners will be sent shrieking to their infernal grave.

The true hedonist must reclaim from Moralist Mark the *descendent* path: the path of earthly delights, the path of sensual pleasure, the path of natural beauty.

The voice of Moralist Mark comes, understandably, as a response to one of the central problems of the pleasure impulse: egoism and destructiveness. If a tyrant or school bully gets pleasure out of inflicting pain on others, which seems to be the case, how can pleasure be part of the solution to the world's problems, as I am suggesting?

What's more, there is a tyrant and a bully in *all* of us. There is a bumptious schoolyard inside our mind; there is a politically unstable country inside us, populated with bullies and their flunkeys. If we don't bully others, then we bully ourselves.

Therefore focusing on our own pleasure would seem to many a dangerous, selfish and even immoral path. The *opposite* of virtue, as Marcus Tullius suggests above.

Isn't it logical then to say there are good pleasures and bad pleasures and we should all steer a course towards the former? Isn't it much safer to base our life on a moral code and thereby protect ourselves, and others, from the pernicious effects of the pleasure impulse?

Two problems:

First, who decides which pleasures are good and which are bad? I remember sitting in a shady bar in Tangier next to an equally shady local who had just persuaded me to buy a carpet I didn't want.

"Look around you, my friend," he gestured, inhaling with gravitas on a big fat joint. "Everyone here is drinking tea. We Moslems do not drink alcohol – that is why we are such a great people."

Second, it is assumed that pleasure and moral action are not connected. There are in fact two types of pleasure derived from moral action. *Ego pleasure* accompanies a feeling of moral superiority (of course it feels good up on the moral high ground) and *soul pleasure* accompanies a genuinely noble action. Soul pleasure is worth going for; ego pleasure is for pleasure lightweights, as we will see.

These problems arise because pleasure is seen as something superficial and self-indulgent. On the contrary, the deepest pleasures come precisely because they are *not* superficial or self-indulgent. In other words, Moralist Mark at his best is *also* being motivated by the pleasure impulse.

As soon as pleasure is approached from a depth-perspective, a perspective of quality, space opens up in the conflict between pleasure and morality. A dialogue can form between the two.

Perhaps Epicurus himself, the grandfather of hedonism and (contrary to what one might expect) hardly a reckless *bon viveur*, can give the best response to Moralist Mark and all those who wish to split pleasure into good and bad or do away with it all together:

"No pleasure is in itself evil, but the things which produce certain pleasures entail annoyances many times greater than the pleasures themselves."

In other words, true hedonism involves discipline and discernment.

Another typical social response to pleasure and one very much one in vogue today in Western culture – and perhaps in reaction to Moralist Mark – is Milly the Mindless Materialist; Mindless Milly for short. Her message is: pleasure lies in possession.

If only I can cherish the latest gadget, emanate the latest perfume, wear the right brand, have a girlfriend with the right shape, drive a fast car, have a thousand Facebook friends…

Mindless Milly thinks she is gaining quality of life from what she buys, but in terms of pleasure she is going merely for quantity and fails to realize that the deeper pleasures come from within. French philosopher Michel Onfray calls this *"hedonisme d'avoir"*, as opposed to a *"hedonisme d'être"* – echoing another famous dictum of Epicurus:

"Not what we have but what we enjoy constitutes our abundance."

This craving to possess beautiful objects (and the imagined pleasure they will bring) is mercilessly exploited by the commercial world, whose intent is not to give us pleasure but to keep us in a continuous state of desire. How wonderful for a materialistic, consumerist society that we never quite get want we want! Through the media, we are titillated and tantalized by a torrent of images of people experiencing unimaginable levels of ecstasy and excitement at possessing or consuming the most trivial things.

There is nothing *wrong* with material possessions and they *do* give some pleasure, but to orient our aspirations, our energy, our very happiness around such things is deeply misguided. If you ask people what gives them *most* pleasure in life – as I have done many times – they will almost *never* refer to material possessions. They will refer to family, to love, to friendship, to achievements, to religion.

And Mindless Milly is in *me*. I hate not having the latest iPhone. I also look with envy at a neighbour's Aston Martin. Mindless Milly is part of our culture, part of our communal world view – and we will either adopt her blindly or rebel against her in a moral fury. Neither reaction will lead to deeper pleasure.

Mindless Milly is also an insatiable *pleasure voyeur*: if she can't have these things herself, then she will at least experience a bittersweet pleasure in seeing others swinging from ecstasy to dejection in their pursuit of the ultimate pleasures. Movies, magazines, pornography, advertisements, they dangle before us unimaginable concoctions of passion, adventure and fulfilment.

This kind of pleasure voyeurism does bring *some* pleasure, but it is mere shadows on the cave wall. The voyeur is permanently envious, dependent on vicarious thrills, never quite satisfied… and spends more money.

A commercial society knows exactly how to exploit Milly: stoke the fires of desire, but withhold pleasure itself; keep pleasure at a tantalean distance. Keep her wanting more…

So far we have seen two forms of reaction to pleasure: suppress it or chase it blindly. There is another: led by Mediocre Mike. Mediocre Mike is a master at *deadening* the pleasure impulse.

It is Mediocre Mike that drove Nietzsche mad and gave birth to his superman. This is where the masses reside in their mediocrity and conformity. Mediocre Mike is the part of ourselves that follows the crowd, that settles for less, that gives far more attention to avoiding the pain of change than seeking real pleasure.

Mediocre Mike will usually have a smile on his face, however plastic. He will do all the right things in life, do his duty: in his family, in his work, in his bed. But he takes no risks. And if he does, the risks are kept secret. He keeps his pleasure impulse on a macrobiotic diet, and he dares not look into the pleasure wasteland behind his routines and rounds of duty. He avoids the very notion of deep pleasure. His pleasure comes chiefly from a stable, socially acceptable identity. But there is no depth, no ecstasy. There is no acute pain either, just a chronic ache and a question in the back of his mind: *Is this all there is?*

Mediocre Mike manifests in me as the robotic father and husband, fulfilling endless tasks, always in a hurry, ticking things off his list. My chief pleasure comes from finishing the list, not from the activities themselves.

I adore my wife and children, but do I really make the best of these relationships? Am I present? Distracted by lists, distracted by junk flow, distracted by a vague 'life is elsewhere' feeling – while right before me is a shining, vibrant child, ready to dive into any stream of contact we choose to create together.

Mediocre Mike can't bear depth; he won't risk angels because he can't bear the thought of the demons that might also come out of the closet. Mediocre Mike is terrified of change. *Don't dig deep. Follow the norms.*

Mediocre Mike keeps smiling, but his twin sister, Masochist Meg, does not. Hers is a gloomy resignation: *Well, I will never get what I* want anyway in life, so better just grind on and gain the little crumbs of satisfaction I can.

One of these crumbs is victimhood: *At least it is not my fault; it's just that I have been dealt a bad hand.*

Out of this joylessness develops cynicism. Then, instead of envy for the happiness of others, the cynic feels contempt and pity for their delusions.

"I may not be happy, but at least I can see through your fake pleasure and happiness! I am brilliant at dissecting others and revealing all their flaws – even my own!"

Another failed marriage, another war, another world disaster… such gloomy events give a grain of satisfaction to cynical Meg. Her gloomy world view is proved correct. She can remain in the comfort of her cynical identity. And, most important of all:

I don't have to make any changes in my life – there is no point, because it is all one big mess anyway.

I see Masochist Meg as a kind of anti-pleasure force that sometimes surfaces in me. Why on earth do I stay in that relationship or that job when I know I am not happy? Negative thoughts about myself and about the world have a subtle, almost hypnotic appeal.

Somewhere in her history, Masochist Meg has been severely disappointed. Her hopes and castles at some point came crashing down and she has never quite recovered. Life has a bitter taste. She prides herself on her 'realism', her ability to apply the cold shower of reality. It gives her a slither of pleasure to bring the castles of others crashing down too – and preempt any new ones she might be tempted to erect for herself.

Like Mediocre Mike, she is afraid of change: afraid of being disappointed again; afraid of reawakening that old wound. Better to stay cynical and safe – no castles, no crashes.

Our last character is Advaita Al – the trickiest by far! Advaita Al has seen through all the other characters. He has been to India and come back with a serious meditation practice.

"Pleasure is not so much wrong as illusory – belonging as it does to the gross realms," is his mantra. Advaita Al is all ascendant. "Rise above the swamp, transcend desire and pleasure. Pleasure belongs to the transient and dualistic world of form."

Advaita Al is after the formless *truth* that is non-dual.

He has a point! As we will see when we explore *spiritual pleasure*, some of the deepest pleasures probably *are* transpersonal and difficult, even pointless, to express in conventional pleasure terms. The problem is that Advaita Al tends to fall into the trap of *judging* and even denying descendent pleasures. He will dismiss the very notion of pleasure – what a mundane, misconceived pursuit! Truth is a much more noble goal. (Not that 'goals' as such have any meaning for him… in theory.)

For Advaita Al, pleasure is not so much the bait of evil as the bait of the ego.

Advaita Al's roots are in Buddhism and other forms of Eastern philosophy and spiritual practice. The Buddha said very clearly: "Desire is the root of all suffering." In other words, you have to work on your relationship to desire, loosen its hold on you and gradually extricate yourself from the swamp.

This teaching makes sense to me and has informed a large part of my life. I have been Advaita Al. I have lived in ashrams, devoted myself to enlightenment, thrown myself wholeheartedly into every meditation and 'worked' on myself to the bone. And I am deeply grateful for all I received and learnt – I am a different person as a result of that immersion.

And I lost my way.

I stopped checking whether I was happy.

In my enthusiasm to ascend and touch the stars, I ignored and even denied the pains in my body and heart. It took me a long time to recover – and neither gurus nor meditation were the answer.

Truth is not my goal any more.

Pleasure is more important to me than truth.

What is the point of 'truth' anyway unless life will somehow please us more when we are enlightened by the truth? The pleasure impulse is absolutely implicit in every religious and spiritual teaching that has ever existed.

The subtext of every teaching is: if you do this, your life will be better (even if that means in the after-life!). Even if the teaching states that you must stop trying to make your life better, the reason you do this is so that your life will become better.

Too strong a truth-orientation leads us astray and denies its own roots in the pleasure impulse. The pursuit of pleasure is regarded with suspicion and aversion by Advaita Al: as *that which is to be transcended*. In this way, humans are encouraged to oppose one of their most basic life forces. Because Eastern religion and spiritual practice are in general less moralistic than Western religion and threaten with endless lifetimes rather than endless infernos, the dismissal of pleasure as a motivating force is much more subtle. Yet pleasure becomes the antithesis of the sacred (or moral), whereas I am placing pleasure at the *core* of the sacred. I am saying that delectation is the meeting point of heaven and earth and when practiced in the right way results in a natural state of gratitude and love.

These are the kind of characters that inhabit both society and our head. These are the kind of voices we have to deal with if we are to tackle the barriers to pleasure. And these voices will *fight* to stay in our head; these voices will *fight* for their cause in society. Their causes can be summed up as follows:

Moralist Mark thinks pleasure will lead us into sin and moral anarchy.

Materialist Milly treats pleasure like a binge-drinking session and embarks on one wild pleasure chase after another.

Mediocre Mike does his duty and stays on the surface of life: he pays lip service to the pleasure impulse, but lives in denial of its deeper, more subversive implications.

Masochist Meg hates the very mention of pleasure, because it reminds her of her basic joyless existence.

Avatar Al doesn't want to muddy his hands in the mire of pleasure, which sucks him down into the sticky world of desire; he prefers to seek truth with a big T.

As an antidote to these characters, here is what the poet Shelley had to say about pleasure and its genesis:

The Birth of Pleasure

At the creation of the Earth
Pleasure, that divinest birth,
From the soil of Heaven did rise,
Wrapped in sweet wild melodies –
Like an exhalation wreathing
To the sound of air low-breathing
Through Aeolian pines, which make
A shade and shelter to the lake
Whence it rises soft and slow;
Her life-breathing [limbs] did flow

In the harmony divine
Of an ever-lengthening line
Which enwrapped her perfect form
With a beauty clear and warm.

Truth and Pleasure
in a Postmodern World

When i was 16 years old, i fell in love with an indian guru.

That sounds erotic – was even erotic and yet not remotely sexual. I was in love!

I attended an optional sixth-form class called 'Who am I?' (a no-brainer for someone like me). At the end of the class I went up to the orange-clad teacher and said: "I have to know more."

When I saw a picture of his guru, I burst into tears.

I read one of his books and my world turned upside down. A veil had been lifted...

English boarding schools are rarely compared to roads to and from Damascus, but that was a huge turning point in my life. Since then my particular spiritual road has taken many more twists and turns, but nothing will take away from the purity and beauty of those first moments – no Freudian analysis, no sociological analysis, no psychobabble of any kind.

Meanwhile, there were mixed responses to the guru stuff back at home.

My mother was vaguely interested, my father pronounced him a scoundrel, and my born-again aunt stated that he was without doubt Satan.

This last attack was my first major brush with Truth with a big T. And I did tremble!

I was a more-or-less practising Christian throughout my childhood, albeit with dangerous liberal tendencies. I had heard enough tales of fire and brimstone to put the fear of God in me. I was enveloped by Guilt with a big G. After sleepless nights I finally went to the school priest to confess my dilemma.

How blessed I have been in my life to hear wise words from wise people at key moments.

"If your heart says follow the guru Rajneesh, then follow your heart," he said.

In that instant, the soul-crushing weight of the capital T was released. I wonder if the priest knew how important his words were.

This was another life-changing moment as I experienced the possibility of more than one truth and the freedom that entails. I was given permission to follow my own knowing.

And I weep at all the Truths that are at this very moment rammed down so many young throats.

Truth with a big T is what they call a meta-narrative: an account of life and the cosmos that is claimed as universal and incontrovertible. In order to highlight the contrast with the pleasure perspective, I am tying moral truth and ontological truth to the same mast. Plato famously divided life into the good, the true and the beautiful: morality, science and aesthetics. I am lumping the good and the true together because they both tend to seek Truth with a big T. There are of course forms of ethics which do point more towards the kind of subjective knowing I am talking about, but there is still a general tendency towards an objective, universal, externalized norm. The contrast – and link – to pleasure is rarely made.

Orthodox religion provides the most obvious examples, but these Truths are not only to be found in holy scriptures: they can be found in science books which claim that everything in the universe can be explained physically; they can be found in political ideologies, racial ideologies, even new-age ideologies.

The advantage of Truth with a big T is that it creates order and unity – among those who espouse that particular Truth. Institutionalized religion, nationalism, communism, imperialism, all these Truths create commonality and offer guidance: this is how the world works, and this is how *you* are meant to work. The quality and consequences of that guidance are of course highly questionable, and each form of commonality will ultimately spawn division.

Life can feel pretty messy and Truths with a big T can give people a sense of clarity and security, as long as they stay within their own bubble of Truth.

The first problem with Truth with a big T is that there is in theory no plural. Everyone claims theirs as the only big T. This makes for uneasy bedfellows. Not surprisingly, Truths from different parts of the world bump up against each other.

We get Truth wars.

The evangelical atheists so vociferous these days are wrong to say religion is the cause of most wars: Truth is the cause of most wars, dogmatic adherence to a particular ideology, including atheism. Religion is just one playing field for the Truth game. Race, political affiliation, almost any kind of strong group identity, can be equally dogmatic and dangerous.

Let us be clear about this: Truth wars have created horrific degrees of suffering for horrific numbers of people. Death, torture, persecution, oppression… history can be seen on one level as a litany of lethal Truth wars. This is true also for the 21st century.

All in the name of Truth: this is our land, ours is the true God, our way is right, we are the superior race.

In less dramatic ways, we are all caught up in Truth wars in almost every aspect of life. Democrats do battle with Republicans, science does battle with religion, creationism does battle with evolution, traditional medicine does battle with alternative medicine, Christianity does battle with Islam, atheism does battle with religion, nature does battle with nurture, and so on.

A truly integrated approach, in which Truths drop their capital T and peacefully co-exist as partial truths, seems far, far away.

A good example of an utterly absurd Truth war in which I became embroiled took place at my university. Despite my early induction into the world of gurus and exotic spirituality, I managed to attend a university of great renown. Dressed in red and purple (to the partial relief of family and friends, the colour scheme for initiates had evolved from orange to any shade of red), and sporting a name of obscure Sanskrit origin, I entered the halls of academia as had been intended for me from an early age.

Back in the eighties, the world of literary criticism to which I belonged resembled a war zone. Militant methodological groups vied for the intellectual high ground. A second Norman invasion had occurred in the form of 'continental' philosophy. Flags with incomprehensible names began to wave from faculty turrets, all of them including the affixes 'post' or 'struct': post-structuralism, deconstruction, constructivism, and so on. Before I knew it, I was caught in the crossfire between the indigenous collaborators and the resistance. And I a poor innocent student who just wanted to party...

Of course I learnt some basic principles of combat: I found out in which camps the intention of the author was paramount and in which camps Heidegger quotes scored highly.

Looking back, I am stunned at the imbecility of this particular Truth war and the inability of partisans to realize what was really going on. What a waste of energy, what a waste of pleasure! How utterly obvious that each methodology contained a partial truth but not the whole Truth – a truth that, ironically, the continental invaders were meant to be bringing! The gap between clever and wise can be considerable.

If only the truth perspective had been softened and deepened by the pleasure perspective and the pleasure of reading and critiquing had equal value to the validity of a particular methodology.

Pleasure takes the destructive bite out of Truth.
Pleasure softens the masculine drive.

Truth wars with a big T are easily visible on a macro level. Truths with small t's are more likely to be seen on the micro level. Even at family level, even within our own mind, we are torn between conflicting views of truth with a small t, conflicting views of how life should be, how we should be, how others should be.

Truths with small t's are the clusters of norms that float between our conscious and unconscious minds, the half-visible drivers of our behaviour. Truths with small t's work like hospital drips, seeping into our bloodstream and guiding our lives without us realizing it. These drips work as anodynes, lulling us into automatic pilot, dulling us to any excess of pain or joy. Truths with a big T can become a matter of life or death, truths with a little t become a matter of physical life and death to the soul: are we asleep or awake?

Attending to pleasure wakes us up and forces us to challenge the truths we have formed about ourselves and life. If we can just for a moment substitute *What is right?* with *What gives us pleasure?*, then there is a opportunity for change. I am not saying abandon the truth perspective altogether, but on its own the truth perspective is too fiery and destructive, or too evangelical and coercive (capital T), or too numbing and paralysing (small t). The pleasure perspective acts as a counter-balance, embraces the feminine, brings us back to the earth of our bodies and wakes us up to our personal reality as we actually experience it, not what we are told to experience.

I am not against Truth. That would be a strange truth to adopt.

I am sceptical.

For the hedonist, the purpose of truth is to liberate: we see a deeper level of truth from which we have been operating and that frees us from certain limitations and enables us to lead a happier life. Truth is not a goal in itself, however, just a means of liberation, an enabler of joy.

Truth with a big T has in fact been under siege since the age of Enlightenment, and is still under siege. Thanks to the second Norman invasion and Postmodern Pete's noble efforts of deconstruction, many of our former towers of Truth in the Western world (and increasingly in the developing world) have crumbled. A postmodern world suggests no absolute Truths, and no sacred cows to fertilize such Truths. Postmodernism has reasserted that man, or rather society and culture, are the measure of all things. Unfortunately, this no-truth is equally absolute and truth-oriented… and fails miserably to make us happier.

Of course, Truth with a big T has fought back.

The postmodern invasion has also provoked a strong backlash in various forms of fundamentalism. New or refurbished towers of Truth have been erected in proud defiance and vigorously defended. God is both dead and very much alive.

In general, however, the relativist, pluralist values informing postmodernism have liberated many people from certain dogmas, from certain truth-and-norm shackles. My Truth has now for many become my truth.

Unfortunately, even truths with a small t can be detrimental to pleasure. Even these truths create clusters of truths-and-norms to which their adherents must conform. Fundamentalist religion is an easy example because of the size of its capital T, but one also sees highly conformist groups of bankers, sportsmen, anarchists, punks, hoodies, greenies…

The problem with the truth perspective is that our point of reference becomes externalized. We live from outside in, guided by the invisible strings of the truths-and-norms that have become our puppet-master.

The pleasure approach works from inside out.

There is no code, only an inner knowing which is in constant evolution.

The truth perspective works from outside in and takes over this inner knowing. Would someone really decide to go and blow themselves and others up if they had been operating from the beginning from their own knowing, from their own subjective sense of right and wrong? Indoctrination happens first: the imposition of Truth.

Or the subtle drip-drip assimilation of truth.

In a stumbling, groping manner, we are already moving away from a truth perspective towards a more individualized, pleasure-based way of looking at the world. Pleasure gets more airspace these days, but this transition is chaotic and visionless hitherto. Too easily one gospel is simply replaced by another (albeit more sexy) gospel, but the reference point remains external. People still operate from outside in.

Pleasure is in the air, but the collective mindset is still oriented to truths-and-norms. Many people in so-called developed societies do give more value and attention to their own pleasure and happiness, but this attention is still guided from outside: *what makes other people happy? What is everyone else doing to bring more pleasure into their lives? What are others doing on TV? What are others doing on Facebook?*

People in general are not anchored in their own pleasure meters.

What ensues is a blind and sometimes gross form of hedonism driven by Mindless Milly. Milly is more interested in quantity and conformity rather than quality. There is little discipline of reflection, little depth of conscious intent.

But there is already a partial movement away from truth and it is that very movement which I am trying to capture and shape in a more constructive form. The movement is still clumsy and even destructive. The movement has yet to connect most of us to our hearts and deeper longings.

Many of the people I come across in my environment (and as voices in my own inner environment) are a mixture of Mediocre Mike and Mindless Milly. The Ms are not so caught up any more in Truths as in truths. Pleasure appears increasingly on the menu, but Mike and Milly are stuck on the starters.

Neither the media nor social media help.

> *Truths with small t's coagulate into a huge wodge of flotsam,*
> *drifting on the ocean of our consciousness:*
> *a polyglot web of half-truths and (mis)information.*

There is no blatant coercion as with Truths with a big T, but the temptation to compare and conform is enormous, without casting a sufficiently sharp empirical eye on our inner state of mind and heart. We are still living our lives too much outside-in as opposed to inside-out.

While visiting the US in the 60s, British writer Christopher Isherwood captured the essence of this phenomenon succinctly in a letter to a friend. By now, of course, the malaise has spread far beyond the US:

"To live sanely in Los Angeles (or, I suppose, in any other large American city) you have to cultivate the art of staying awake. You must learn to resist (firmly but not tensely) the unceasing hypnotic suggestions of the radio, the billboards, the movies and the newspapers; those demon voices which are forever whispering in your ear what you should desire, what you should fear, what you should wear and eat and drink and enjoy, what you should think and do and be. They have planned a life for you — from the cradle to the grave and beyond — which it would be easy, fatally easy, to accept. The least wandering of the attention, the least relaxation of your awareness, and already the eyelids begin to droop, the eyes grow vacant, the body starts to move in obedience to the hypnotist's command. Wake up, wake up — before you sign that seven-year contract, buy that house you don't really want, marry that girl you secretly despise. Don't reach for the whiskey, that won't help you. You've got to think, to discriminate, to exercise your own free will and judgment. And you must do this, I repeat, without tension, quite rationally and calmly. For if you give way to fury against the hypnotists, if you smash the radio and tear the newspapers to shreds, you will only rush to the other extreme and fossilize into defiant eccentricity."

We are, I believe, in no-woman's land at this time, stuck between the old and the new. The traditional towers of truth have either been nuked or resurrected in a frighteningly dogmatic way, but, generally speaking, we haven't fully individuated and found our own truth. We are still only half awake, lost in the mist of half-conscious truths-and-norms. And our own truth needs to be connected to pleasure. Postmodern society talks the talk of individualization, but it doesn't deliver the walk.

We need a guiding mechanism that is pragmatic and at the same time honours you and me as separate individuals. We need a compass which includes the *What's in it for me?* subtext that permeates our society – and rightly so. Each person's personal happiness is important. The sacred cows we previously served can no longer cow many of us into the subservience of our own personal needs.

In this sense the hedonism I am suggesting is not utilitarian: I am not prioritizing the happiness of the majority over the happiness of the few. I am saying each individual happiness is important and I am challenging the notion that there is only room in the world for so many 'happinesses'! If there can be a general movement away from ego pleasures then there is enough pleasure for everyone – because the deeper pleasures in life involve loving and serving others.

Pleasure is available to everyone. Pleasure is pragmatic in the sense that it is tangible. Pleasure gives us both a goal and a means of evaluating whether that goal has been reached. Pleasure also honours our individuality – indeed it has meaning only in relation to our inner felt sense. No other person, book or doctrine can ultimately decide or measure what gives us pleasure.

I hear the cry: "But this will lead to yet more rampant greed and individualism and the further decline of society!"

It will lead to a purer form of individualism. Rampant, no. What we have now is not real individualism because people haven't really individuated. Yes, many of the towers of Truth have crumbled, many traditional shackles loosened, but now we are chained to a mass market of superficial pleasure and empty promises of joy. Mindless Milly has entered the stage. Genuine individuation requires a profound emancipatory process, one that frees us from our upbringing, from all our shoulds and shouldn'ts, from all the new half-truths that are being peddled at the media market. We have to answer the question *What really makes me happy?* and not *What do others say will make me happy?*

The discipline of pleasure doesn't lead to rampant anything, especially individualism, for so many pleasures come from human contact and community.

When you ask people what gives them pleasure, they almost always point to soul pleasures (see chapter 5c) – love for children, being successful, contributing to the success of others, friendship, and so on. The world is scared of pleasure, the word has a dirty name, because people think it is related to dissipation and excess. The whole point of the new hedonism is to bring breadth and depth to pleasure and rescue it from the clutches of the moralists and materialists.

I believe that the time when people can easily accept external truths and follow them to the letter are over, though a few hard-core fanatics caught in a time warp remain. It's too much hard work, too much swimming against the current of the times. Most people don't believe enough any more and even if they do they don't have the kind of discipline needed to put those beliefs into practice.

Yeats's famous dictum could not be more relevant:

"The best lack all conviction, while the worst are full of passionate intensity."

The postmodern world needs a softer from of discipline that fits the trends of the time:

"Be yourself."

"What's in it for me?"

"I want to find my own way."

"I want to have a good time…"

We are the 'me-me' generations, for better or worse, and I believe it is wiser to find a compass that aligns with that movement rather than fights it.

A truth perspective will stress duty, obligation and morality. A pleasure paradigm will stress happiness. The former also (unconsciously) strives for happiness, but the pleasure impulse becomes so clogged up by the shoulds and shouldn'ts of the truth perspective that the quest for happiness is corrupted.

That's a lot to swallow: undigested ideas of morality will corrupt the proper pursuit of pleasure! I hear the cries of protest already: What a monstrous inversion of right and wrong! Society will fall apart!

Well, society already is falling apart.

A Pleasure Typology:
The Different Pleasures

My pleasure typology is only of any use if it helps people to find greater pleasure in their lives. The typology is not an end in itself. Nor is it an attempt to create a genuine ontology of pleasure to be attested by neuroscientists or philosophers. Its purpose is purely pragmatic. The typology goes like this:

Ego, *simple*, *soul* and *spirit*.

Others far more qualified and distinguished than me have created pleasure distinctions and categories – Plato, Epicurus and John Stuart Mill to mention but a few – and though logical enough, none of them really matches my experience. Either the distinctions reflect moral or even social norms or there is little notion of depth.

Jeremy Bentham, the grandfather of utilitarianism (a branch of philosophy often associated with hedonism), famously said:

"Prejudice apart, the game of push-pin is of equal value with the arts and sciences of music and poetry." (For push-pin, think Call of Duty.)

I like the way Bentham levels the playing field and pricks the bubble of moral or social superiority, but why should the value of an act not lie in the depth of pleasure?

There is a hierarchy to my pleasure experiences, based on depth. And the depth of pleasure depends largely on the depth of me, the subject. If I am operating from my ego, I will have less pleasure than when I am operating from my soul. Simple pleasure is necessary and wonderful, but does not have the same depth as spiritual pleasure.

In other words, the external trigger of pleasure is not as important as the internal state of the subject. We tend to think of pleasure as merely the result of an external stimulus – which is why we keep seeking the same stimuli, long after they have exhausted their potential for pleasure. You might call such a predicament *addiction*.

Addiction yields little pleasure because it is coming from the part of us that is trapped: a small self, if you like. Soul pleasure is greater because it comes from a bigger and better part of us.

Take sex for example. Freud is not the only one to suggest that sex is the greatest source of pleasure – the message is screamed out through almost every kind of media today. But the depth of pleasure afforded by sex depends enormously on the inner state and motivation of those involved.

Sex as conquest.

Sex as unlimited love.

Sex as relief.

Sex as release.

Sex as revenge.

Sex as aggression.

Sex as compensation.

Sex as heaven.

Sex as meditation.

Sex as experimentation.

Sex as self-destruction.

Sex as there is nothing better to do.

I have probably tried all of these and their various combinations at some time or other. Each time I make love there is a different inner state for me and a different shared inner state for us. Different motivations, different shared cultures of meaning, different energy. The level of pleasure varies hugely – dependent on my inner world, dependent on my partner's inner world, dependent on our shared inner world.

And the general trend in my life is that sex has become better and better. Because the person who makes love has changed. Skill and technique is but a small part of the learning process. The real work has been on my inner world.

Of course how you do it is important, but even more important is *who* does it. What is the quality of consciousness behind the one who makes love? Is the inner world of those making love so spacious and porous that it can actually include the other in an energetic seamless whole?

When Plato says that sexual pleasure is distinct from and inferior to mental pleasure, I cannot help but wonder what his experience of sex is. If he is referring to a quick heave-ho with a student behind the olive tree, I understand his hierarchy.

Most pleasure typologies follow, like Plato's, a rough division according to the activity involved: the physical, the aesthetic, and the ideal (mental). Though I understand the convenience of dividing pleasure according to its context, it is hard to match this division with my actual experience.

Sex presumably falls under the physical category, but sex without aesthetic seems impoverished to me. Or when I look with the pleasure of love at my son playing and laughing with his friends, I feel not just emotion but warmth in my body. When I hear a particularly moving piece of music, I get goose bumps, shivers of pleasure rippling through my body. My 'spirit' soars and dives...

The deeper pleasures especially seem to involve all of me. Or rather however much of me is available. The more space inside me, the less blocked I am inside, the more pleasure I can feel.

The activity itself does not determine the depth of pleasure so much as the inner state of the subject.

A young Zen student was once asked to take an evening stroll with the master and his senior disciples. At a certain point, the young student remarked, "Look, what a lovely sunset!" He wasn't asked again.

It is one thing to enjoy seeing a sunset, it is quite another thing to feel at one with the sunset – and the latter is in no way enhanced by commenting on it. That is the difference between simple and spiritual pleasure. We will only feel at one with the sunset if the quality of our awareness, our state as subject, permits it.

Take golf as another (deeply spiritual) example. I remember the famous golfer Ian Woosnam once saying that maybe it was time for him to stop because he didn't really enjoy playing golf any more, only winning.

Golf itself does not emit a certain level of pleasure, not even 'good' golf. The pleasure thermometer is sensitive to the inner world of the subject. Woosnam had changed as a person over the years.

Ego is a shallow subject who will experience shallow pleasure. And shallow is not the same as bad. My typology does not represent a moral hierarchy whereby spiritual pleasure is better than simple pleasure. It is just more pleasurable.

By removing the moral hierarchy to pleasure, however, that does not mean there should be no hierarchy. Hierarchy creates difference of depth or degree and only causes problems when one level of the hierarchy tries to dominate another. Without any sense of depth, we are left with a flat world inhabited by flat people. The hedonism I am espousing is about depth of subject, depth of pleasure.

The pleasure typology presented here is based on the state of being, the state of consciousness of the subject: who we are when we have the pleasure. How much pleasure we have depends on who we are. The pleasure impulse is non-discriminatory: it will find its inevitable way into all parts of us, into whoever we are at any given moment. The rest is up to us.

Ego Pleasures

I HAVE HAD A FIGHT WITH MY PARTNER. AS I STORM OUT of the room, rampant with righteous anger, I imagine how long I will snub her after this. And guess what? Yes, the thought gives me some pleasure. The truth underneath is that I am hurting – and the pleasure impulse immediately kicks in: damage limitation. Unfortunately, the state I am in – and possibly the stage of emotional development I am in – is such that the only way of reducing the suffering is through an ego pleasure: a thought of revenge; a plan to make my partner suffer as I am. I will show her!

Or you are a bit jealous of a colleague – she may rise further than you. In a meeting you manage to put her down with a sharp quip that confuses and upsets her. You feel a little thrill of power at seeing her temporarily powerless. Admit it: it feels good! Briefly.

Later you feel some remorse, which is pain, the opposite of pleasure. The next day, as she refuses to meet your eye, you feel another prick of discomfort. Even if you don't feel any remorse, you will tighten when you see her again. You will feel a tension in your body, a contraction in her presence. You may have to brace yourself to maintain your hardness.

In the next meeting, you may feel more confident on one level, but you will also be wary and watchful. Your pride may be in tact, but you will also feel closed and hardened. And you are probably unaware that the greatest pleasure may come through saying sorry and creating a deeper form of contact: a soul pleasure.

The ego pleasure may well win out though. Shame. For you, as well as for her. You are settling for scraps of pleasure.

Ego pleasure is largely a mental creation; very little release or flow is felt physically; indeed the opposite is true. By ego, I refer not to the Freudian concept of ego, but to a *distorted self-image*: an inflated or deflated self-image. In common usage, ego implies the inflated image: "What a big ego he has!"

In my twenty years experience in the fields of self-development and organizational change I have noticed that people can have an equally big ego (meaning distortion) in the opposite direction; namely deflation. "I am useless" is just as much an ego-based reaction as "I am the best". Both are fear based, both are a chronic reaction to pain, both distort our behaviour and cause us to manipulate our environment in a way harmful both to ourselves and others.

We act from ego when we boost our self-image at the expense of others or diminish our self-image (at our own expense). These are pleasures that generally involve harming ourselves or others.

But how can self-destructive behaviour be linked to pleasure?

I have said the other side of the pleasure coin is avoiding pain – and here is an example of *seeking* pain. How can seeking pain be linked to the pleasure impulse?

It is about 'victimhood'.

The idea and even the identity of being a victim brings a certain comfort. Inflicting pain upon ourselves can be a means of proving certain convictions we have: I am bad, other people are bad, life is bad. This brings a kind of solace.

Taking a victim stance has many advantages: the victim is beyond criticism, the victim always deserves pity, the victim doesn't need to be held accountable for what happens.

Victimhood generally starts with genuine acts of oppression. There is an oppressor and an oppressed. I do not take the grossly solipsistic view so fashionable in the New Age movement that we create entirely our own reality. We also simply get blessed and whacked in life. Genetics, family and cultural history, and just plain being in the wrong place at the wrong time are all factors outside our control.

Victimhood, though, is a state of mind that goes beyond specific events. Victimhood is a coat of armour adopted to cope with the whacks. Adorning such a coat of armour is understandable and the victim deserves our compassion in so far as we can empathize with the original pain and its consequences.

Victimhood is a coping mechanism that works in the sense that it offers some comfort. The pleasure impulse manages to wrangle its way even into such a bleak picture… but the comfort is pale.

To make matters worse, the oppressor becomes internalized and we begin to oppress ourselves, do ourselves harm, reinforce destructive patterns. Such self-oppression is not always conscious, but it is unmistakeable in our actions and the kind of situations we attract: the painful truth is that the one who has been abused will seek out or attract further abusive situations.

The horror of this vicious circle is, I imagine, familiar to us all to different degrees. For those who have been victims of severe oppression, the circle is deeper and more poignant.

The fact is we beat ourselves up.

Emotionally, we torture ourselves with criticism and self-mockery. Physically we subject our body to various degrees of abuse, from over-eating or mild alcoholism to self-mutilation. We *all* choose at some point or other to stay in dysfunctional patterns. How many times have we looked at friends, colleagues or clients and thought: *Why on earth do they do that? Why do they bring such grief on themselves?* How many times have our friends looked at us in the same way, with the same mixture of frustration and pity?

Beating ourselves up strengthens our victimhood and gives us a twisted sense of satisfaction. The only way out of the hell and towards deeper levels of comfort and pleasure is by working off the suit of armour and releasing ourselves from the constrictions of victimhood.

The only pleasure this coat of armour can give is ego pleasure – the lowest rung on the pleasure ladder.

Acting with discipline and working on ourselves is a means of creating more potential for pleasure. Perhaps Michel Foucault had similar thoughts:

"What we must work on, it seems to me, is not so much to liberate our desires but to make ourselves infinitely more susceptible to pleasure."

More diversity of pleasure, more depth of pleasure.

There are two bold and terrible truths about ego pleasure to be faced.

First we have to admit and confront the devil and saboteur in us; the part of us that enjoys hurting others and the part of us that enjoys hurting ourselves. It is easier to assume we are innocent and others are guilty. It is easy to see evil in others but not in ourselves. This realization is in fact a double whammy: not only do we think and do bad things to ourselves and others, but we actually enjoy it!

Of course, the lure of ego-boosting pleasures appear to make more sense than those that involve ego-diminishment, but both are just as real. Both forms of ego pleasure are the result of some basic pain and discomfort within us. The pleasure impulse pushes us towards some kind of compensation or relief from this pain – either through self-aggrandizement or through self-diminishment. Being top dog or bottom dog gives us temporary relief.

People tend to judge the pleasure of top-dog mentality (self-aggrandizement) more severely because the pleasure comes at the expense of others: the strutting bully is an easier target for our disapproval than the stooped whinger.

Such a judgement is misleading, however. The two forms of ego pleasure are different sides of the same coin and both arise from the same basic pain of not feeling good enough. Both cause suffering to those around them. The self-pitying victim is also painful and frustrating to be around. Self-harm harms others too. The subtext of the victim is: "I will make you suffer through witnessing my suffering. And when I see you suffering with my suffering, I feel a tiny bit better."

The second realization is to see that this ego pleasure, this level of enjoyment, is paltry; the pleasure yield is meagre and unsustainable. Ego pleasure often leads to greater pain in the end. This is where the discipline of pleasure kicks in: daring to look objectively at the pleasure scales. How happy are we really at the end of the day?

The main reason we don't dare to look objectively at the pleasure scales is because we fear change: if we see clearly the depth of our pain and the flimsiness of our pleasure, we know that change is the only sane option. And that change may well involve first going deeper into the underlying pain. We would rather stay in the now familiar shelter of our semi-misery. At least in that way we avoid the risk of new hopes for pleasure that might end in further pain and disappointment.

So even the refusal to look objectively at our lives, even the denial of our true condition, is connected to the pleasure impulse: we are protecting ourselves from our original pain and suffering. However, the price we pay for this self-protection – which may have served a good purpose at some stage in our lives – brings a heavy reduction in our potential for pleasure. The armour we have adopted deadens our pleasure receptors and prevents deeper forms of pleasure.

Until we recognize these uncomfortable truths and understand the essential neutrality and inevitability of the pleasure impulse, we will be cruel and unforgiving both to ourselves and others. We are often unaware that even a modicum of pleasure does come from ego games. I don't believe we ever genuinely do, or even can, seek purely pain and suffering – there is always some edge of pleasure that is being sought through the pain.

The vicious circles of ego pleasure can be broken with the help of two qualities: heartfelt *compassion* and ice-clear *objectivity*. Feeling our own pain and that of others, seeing the damage and the need for change. First a melting of the pain, a release from the lonely armour, balm to the wounds, then an uncompromising look at what has happened and what can happen.

Ego pleasures are scraps to our pleasure appetite, never a whole meal. They are unfulfilling, but enough to keep us going. And often, even for long periods of our lives, we are prepared to feed on scraps. It is pleasure on a boot-string, pleasure at survival level.

Ego pleasures don't run deep, but they are reliable in the sense that they are familiar and they are not hard to attain. The move from ego pleasures into more satisfying pleasures involves *risk*. We may have to change and grow in order to bring deeper pleasure into your life. We may have to give up certain parts of our identity, certain areas of safety and familiarity.

For the tyrant who gains ego pleasure from domination and even cruelty, the move to an orientation around deeper forms of pleasure will require vulnerability and the courage to go through his darkest fears and insecurities.

For the victim to wrench herself out of the victim role and start believing in her own worth is hard, scary work – and might force her to make significant changes in her life.

Sweat and tears for both. The only way out is through… to a greater capacity for joy on the other side.

Simple Pleasures

"*The happiness of life is made up of minute fractions – the little, soon-forgotten charities of a kiss or smile, a kind look, a heartfelt compliment, and the countless infinitesimals of pleasurable and genial feeling.*"
– Samuel Taylor Coleridge

I am in a small hotel in a cold Berlin.

I have to get up in the middle of the night to go the toilet, and stagger, eyes half-closed, into the tiny bathroom. I don't turn the light on – to avoid the glare – and walk slowly, groping, towards the toilet. I feel warm tiles under my feet. For a while I just sit there on the toilet, feeling the warmth of the floor-heating ebb through the soles of my feet, spreading through tingling toes. For a few delicious moments, the warmth is *pure pleasure*: all that exists is that golden energy seeping through my body.

Of all the places (and of all the times) to arrive at pleasure!

And just imagine how good the bladder release felt after that…

When it comes to simple pleasures, we are not talking just about picture-book sunsets and Ferraris; we are also talking about dark bathrooms in the middle of the night.

Our bodies and brain open us up to an astonishing array of delights as our senses brush against a world profligate in its sumptuous offerings of sound, colour, smell and touch.

Simple pleasure can come out of the blue, effortless, and superfluous to the demands of everyday life. Simple pleasures are a luxury: we don't need them to survive. Most of us are miserly when it comes to allowing ourselves these luxuries, suspicious even of them… as if they might distract us from what life is really about.

Simple pleasures usually involve the senses and happen as a result of simple interactions with our environment. The meeting of inner and outer. The song of the swallow grazes my ear and enters my inner world, caresses my consciousness. And if my interior world is receptive enough the result can be pleasure.

Such pleasures are available in their myriads if we are only awake and hospitable enough to them. Brushing our teeth, the sound of the birds singing, a surprise smile on the train… any number of small events can flip us into a state of enjoyment. Just like that!

Simple pleasure starts in the body. It is possible that pleasure precedes conscious contact with our environment and is simply a consequence of feeling alive. Sometimes my son skips gleefully around for no apparent reason, singing and delighting like a dolphin in the waves before he even looks for pleasure. Even after an upset, he seems to settle back quite easily into a basic state of pleasurable being. My theory is that it feels good to him just to be alive, and that 'feel-good' is located in his body. In my experience, if a child's basic needs are met (which is sadly not always the case), they are basically happy.

Sometimes I fantasize that pleasure is even more fundamental: the fragrance of consciousness itself, a by-product that makes life worth living, a blessing to sweeten the bitter cup of life we are given that is planted in the DNA of the universe from the beginning.

Whatever the ultimate ontological status of pleasure, it is outrageous how much of the simple pleasure available in life we ignore. The window of opportunity to enjoy these pleasures is often short and unexpected. Indeed the pleasures themselves are often short, ephemeral (and therefore perhaps not valued as much as they should be). If we are not alert enough, we will simply miss the "countless infinitesimals" – the song of the swallows, the sunlight of a smile; I would hardly notice the warmth of the floor in my hotel bathroom. Simple pleasures demand first and foremost that we be awake.

Nobody seems to capture the ephemeral beauty and unpredictability of simple pleasures quite like Coleridge and the other romantic poets. Here is a poem aptly named 'Hidden Joys' by Victorian poet Laman Blanchard:

Hidden Joys

Pleasures lie thickest where no pleasures seem:
There's not a leaf that falls upon the ground
But holds some joy, of silence, or of sound,
Some sprite begotten of a summer dream.
The very meanest things are made supreme
With innate ecstacy. No grain of sand
But moves a bright and million-peopled land,
And hath its Edens and its Eves, I deem.
For Love, though blind himself, a curious eye
Hath lent me, to behold the hearts of things,
And touch'd mine ear with power. Thus, far or nigh,
Minute or mighty, fix'd or free with wings,
Delight from many a nameless covert sly
Peeps sparkling, and in tones familiar sings.

What stops us from being awake to all the "countless infinitessimals"?

What prevents us from "beholding the heart of things"? Habit of thought and action.

Grinding along the same neural pathways day after day, thinking thoughts we have had a thousand times before, kidding ourselves that the same thoughts will still bring something new into our lives.

Going through the motions of life, robotic routine, simply ticking things off our list as fast as possible. In these days of speed and results, we often live like prostitutes to pleasure: get each experience over as quickly as possible so we can move on to our next client.

As the philosopher Kierkegaard once said: "Most men pursue pleasure with such breathless haste that they hurry past it."

Simple pleasures are the flowers we often miss beside the busy road of our oh-so-important lives. I shall never forget working with a group in Santa Fe, New Mexico. We were in the middle of a heated discussion over some project or other when a Native American woman who had barely uttered a word all session suddenly said: "The flowers are listening to us."

There was a vase of flowers in the middle of the circle. The whole vibration in the room changed after that statement. Everything slowed down, people spoke more respectfully; the flowers were present in the circle.

Breaking these habits of thought and action, however, is far from easy. We are swimming against the stream not only of our own habit, but also of a whole culture of habit.

We are asleep among sleepy people.

Watch a small child or a dog when you go out for a walk: the aliveness, the spontaneity, the utter surrender to the moment. Alertness is not enough. Coleridge expresses this far better than I can:

Dejection: An Ode

Those stars, that glide behind them or between,
Now sparkling, now bedimmed, but always seen:
Yon crescent Moon, as fixed as if it grew

In its own cloudless, starless lake of blue;
I see them all so excellently fair,
*I **see**, not **feel**, how beautiful they are!"* [my bold]

Being alert is just the first step.

Pleasure is a felt experience. A certain inner receptivity is also needed. It is as if our pleasure channels need to be open and unblocked, so we can *feel* the event in our veins.

When I feel the warmth of the sun on my skin, to enjoy that warmth,
I need to give it space in my mind and body, let it touch me.
I let the event enter me in order to gain full pleasure.
I need to absorb and savour the full taste of the experience.
I have to surrender to the experience, otherwise it will just bounce off
me, leaving me untouched.

A modern guru who more than any other has managed to combine the spiritual with the sensual and to extricate religion from its renunciatory, ascetic (some might say anti-pleasure) history has this to say:

"Everything is beautiful if inside our heart there is awareness." Osho's use of the word *heart* is interesting. This suggests an awareness that is deeper than the mental, more like loving attention. Most simple pleasures are slices of love and beauty mixed, moments that weave the amorous with the aesthetic. I am drawn to the Romantic poets as they seem particularly aware of this connection between beauty and pleasure. Seeing is not enough, pleasure is a *felt* experience, a sensual experience. No wonder Keats spoke of a "pleasure thermometer".

The good news is the super-abundance of simple pleasure on offer.

The bad news, as with most pleasures, is what philosophers call the 'pleasure paradox'. Put simply, the more we chase pleasure, the more we won't get it. On the other hand, if we go to sleep and forget pleasure, we will also not get it.

If pleasure becomes too much of a goal, this can be counter-productive. The simple pleasures are the flowers beside the road of our usual daily routine that we fail to notice or feel. If those flowers become too much of a goal in themselves then we have simply created another road.

The receptivity I am talking about requires a more subtle, less results-driven attitude. It is more a state of being, an openness to life. Flirting with the outside world, but not chasing or seeking to dominate it in any way. If we are intent on chasing pleasure, we will lack the receptivity to let pleasure in. The drive will come more from our mind than our heart. Awareness of the heart does not depend on action but on alertness *and* receptivity, a state of being rather than doing.

Doing is often contrasted with thinking: the former being active and the latter passive. I experience thinking as another form of doing, but one that happens on the inside rather than on the out-side. The kind of pleasure you can think your way towards, through your imagination, does of course give some satisfaction, but this satisfaction is like the shadows in Plato's cave, or like watching it on TV. It is not the real thing. The real thing is felt more keenly in our bodies and yields a deeper pleasure.

The "countless infinitessimals" of pleasure are guests in our inner home, but if we wish to enjoy their company we have to play host. We have to open the door of our hearts and welcome them in. If we put up a notice saying 'Do not disturb' because we are too busy with the same old thoughts we have had for the past year, or too busy with the same old list of tasks as last weekend, not only do we cut ourselves off from the outside world, we cut ourselves off from simple pleasure.

The host is the subject and the subject must be receptive to pleasure. Subject refers to the whole interior world that enables us to say we are alive, the same inner world that gave birth to Descarte's famous '*cogito ergo sum*'. It is quite clear if you read his further explanations that his 'cogito' does not only refer to mental activity but to the whole phenomenon of consciousness. The only thing he could be sure of in the end was the fact that he had an interior world: that he could be in reflection.

Through working on that interior world, through working on ourselves as subject, we can increase our capacity for joy.

Nowhere is the need to work on our interior world more apparent than in our contact with people. Contact with the world of objects, from nature to wine to a sports car, is in some ways an easier source of simple pleasure. When it comes to others, we tend to have more layers of defence. Yet we have to be able to reach out, or allow others to reach out to us. We are more afraid of the other drivers on the road than the flowers beside the road.

A warm hug, the sound of a friend's voice on the phone during hard times, the giggle of a child, a smile shared between two strangers on a plane, holding a partner's hand as you cross the street: the range of pleasurable contact between human beings is vast. At our best we meet each other: we play, we reassure, we comfort, we fence, we tease, we touch, we stroke, we sympathize, we joke, we share, we flirt.

Another kind of simple pleasure, one that so often fails to penetrate our defences, is taking pleasure in the pleasure of others, enjoying the happiness of others. So simple, so immediate! And so difficult, apparently. In order to free ourselves up for this pleasure

THE DISCIPLINE OF PLEASURE

infection we have to be coming from a place of what used to be called in the therapeutic world: 'I'm okay, you're okay.'

If I am 'not okay', I will be indifferent to or envious of the pleasure of others. If I see you as 'not okay', then I will judge your pleasures, scorn your pleasures.

To arrive at the place of 'I'm okay, you're okay' requires more of that work on the interior world – clearing out the ego cobwebs, cleaning the vessel of our selves.

Although the deeper forms of human contact belong to soul pleasure, there is more than enough on offer in the simple realm.

Think for a moment of our contact with the (rest of the) animal world. Can you really feel quite so miserable when your dog wags his tail and nuzzles up to you? Can you really take life so seriously when you see a cow staring at you with deep, soft, curious eyes?

We miss these simple pleasure opportunities again and again, either because we are too sleepy or too guarded.

Above all, a certain innocence is needed to experience simple pleasure. The kind of innocence that cherishes the ordinary.

Soul Pleasures

THE BASIC MOTTO OF SOUL PLEASURE IS: *life is what you make it.*

Soul pleasure arises from *creating* a good life: working on life, playing with life, tinkering with life, improving life.

The doctor in Haiti (quoted at the start of the book)… his is an example of soul pleasure. He didn't want to be anywhere else in the world. In Haiti, he could both use his expertise (earned through hard work) and live out his deepest values. There he could fulfil his mission, sing the song he was meant to sing.

Soul pleasure is the sense of fulfilment that comes from a life of meaning. Soul pleasures stem from an 'I' at its best, ego pleasures stem from an 'I' at its worst. The 'I' of both ego and soul is connected to agency: what we choose to do or not to do in our lives; what we make of our lives. The nature of this 'I', the quality of the subject, however, determines the quality of action and subsequent level of pleasure.

Ego pleasures may be easier to attain, but soul pleasures yield deeper, more sustainable pleasure. Has not every parent given this message to their children in some form or other?

Before we start, let's not get into a tangle over the word soul. I use the word fairly loosely to describe the best part of us, the noble part of us.

When I imagine my soul, I see the owner of my aspirations and values and I see the seeker, the seat of learning within me. My soul represents the bigger picture, the underlying thread that gives meaning to my path through life. How much that meaning

       THE DISCIPLINE OF PLEASURE

is determined by transpersonal forces (religious) and how much by personal forces (existentialist) is not important to me. I am pragmatic in this: whatever works.

I don't really mind whether my soul transmigrates, reincarnates or joins the angels (best-case scenario) or whether my soul is simply my own attempt (or that of my culture) to imbue my life with meaning.

In my book, soul is not the same as spirit.

Soul is *personal*: my soul is different from yours and follows a different path. Spirit is impersonal: it is the same for all of us, across the universe.

My fantasy is that soul is more personal than spirit and more profound than personality. Soul hovers somewhere between personality and spirit; there is a sense of 'I' but that 'I' is much more spacious and generous than that of the personality or ego.

If you like, soul can be used as a metaphor to signify the best in us.

Gurdjeff, the famous and controversial Russian spiritual teacher, said we have to "grow our own soul". Unlike spirit, the soul is not a given, waiting to be revealed. The soul is a potential that needs to be nurtured and challenged into form. Learning is the water that feeds the plant of the soul.

Growing one's own soul means charting a meaningful trajectory through life: a trajectory that will fulfil our deepest potential. In Gurdjeff's cosmology, the deepest potential is spiritual, but for many people the world of spirit is not their orientation. This does nothing to diminish the kind of noble, meaningful life they can create. Perhaps this is also what Michel Foucault had in mind when he said: "The idea of the bios (life) as a material for an aesthetic piece of art is something that fascinates me. In our society, art has become something that is related only to objects and not to individuals or to life… art is something which is specialized or done by experts who are artists. But couldn't everyone's life become a work of art?"

Perhaps growing our own soul and fashioning a good life for ourselves is the ultimate creative act: to paint the picture of our life, to write our own story, to sing our own song in the world.

Simple and spirit pleasures arise from a sense of acceptance of life and the world exactly as they are: behold, taste, merge and enjoy. Soul pleasure, however, comes through fashioning the kind of life to which we aspire. Career, family, projects, relationships: how can we fulfil our deepest longings and live to our deepest values? Then we will feel pleasure of the soul.

Soul pleasures include the pleasures of loyalty, of being a good parent or good partner, of serving one's country, of accomplishing a mission, of self-sacrifice. While reading Nelson Mandela's autobiography, I sometimes felt envious of the pleasure he must derive (even during the worst phases of his life) from the integrity and nobility of his actions. I also noted that his greatest pain was that he could not be the best possible father or husband. That particular soul pleasure was denied him for many years through the choices he consistently made.

Let us examine soul pleasure through two different aspects of the soul: the *playful soul* and the *virtuous soul*.

THE PLAYFUL SOUL

My work is running workshops and seminars. I help people to change: individuals, groups, organizations, and by extension society in a small way. What I do is congruent with my mission in life: assisted, conscious evolution. I try to help people (including myself), and groups of people, become happier. My mission faces inwards towards myself as well as outwards towards others – I can't really differentiate between the two and don't want to.

I spend a lot of time sitting with circles of people, capturing the wisdom that emerges and translating that wisdom into change. Every circle, every group exploration, feels like an act of creativity to me: a work of art created by me and the group. We are all surfers on the group sea – I just tend to pick the waves a bit earlier.

I have my bad days. I bump up against myself, I bump up against cynicism, against apathy, against a cruel society. But the bottom line is that I do what I love and I love what I do. My trade and my mission are more or less one.

This makes me happy. My soul drinks its fill.

It took me a long time to find what I really wanted to do, to find my particular song. For many years I was interested only in simple and spirit pleasures. The soul dimension was not clear to me. Work was a means to an end, a way of making money to do what I really wanted to do. Then in my early thirties came a shift: I wanted to create something, build something, achieve something. And that project is still evolving.

For many years, ever since I fell in love with literature at school, I have also wanted to write a book; my soul has always enjoyed playing with words. The problem was I never had much to write about until the pleasure theme began to grow in me. Some will say I still don't have much to write about, but I don't think that will worry my soul. This book is in the first place an expression of my soul at play.

I mentioned that my mission is to make a contribution to conscious evolution. I believe the pleasure lens will help this mission and that in turn gives me pleasure.

Before it all sounds too serious and pompous, let me repeat that my mission is essentially a form of play.

Over-seriousness and over-zealousness rarely bring pleasure to anyone, while lightness of touch need not preclude commitment and devotion. My soul is doing its thing, my soul is singing its song, my soul is committed. Work and play are one at a soul level.

I believe the soul starts its training in infancy: reaching out, crawling, walking, touching, tasting, exploring, trying to master the environment. This is why the concept of play is so important. These experiments are different from the simple pleasures of cuddles and milk. These experiments are the first yearnings towards agency, the early struggles to create.

Later in life our aspirations and ambitions become more sophisticated, but that whole movement of the soul starts with an irresistible urge to reach out and touch the world, a need to explore and discover, a sense of wonder, a deep curiosity.

With curiosity comes learning and with learning, creativity. Learning is a form of creativity.

I remember the satisfaction my son derived from learning to read: the first time he could decipher the scrawl on the cereal packet before him on the kitchen table. What a smile accompanied this discovery – as if some obscure hermaneutic secret had been revealed! If only Kellogg's knew how important their texts are…

The ability to learn and create keeps us alive.

By this I don't mean survival – though it may originate there – but alive in terms of energy and vibrancy. Old age becomes a burden only when learning stops. Those who keep learning in their later years seem to retain their life sparkle.

There are many elementary examples of the soul at play: cleaning the house, fixing a broken chair, doing a crossword puzzle, painting a bedroom. These are all creative ways in which we interact with our environment. We are using our creative muscles. When I work in the garden I never fail to feel better afterwards. Some small part of the soul is at play. We are creating a more beautiful environment, we are caring for the environment, we are testing our wits against the environment, we are solving problems in our environment.

The more absorbed we are in the action, the greater the pleasure. The other determining factor of *depth* of pleasure is the depth of meaning attached to the activity.

At the deepest end of the soul spectrum lies *mission*: fulfilling the purposes we create for ourselves or believe we are destined to fulfil.

Cooking a meal at home is one thing. Opening a restaurant that gives simple pleasure to thousands is something more; both are examples of the soul at play, but the latter will tend to yield a deeper pleasure because of the extent of the achievement involved. There is greater meaning to the action.

The word mission may conjure up visions of grandeur that can be unhelpful. We don't have to be a Nelson Mandela to experience soul pleasure. We all act within our own particular life context, created both by circumstance and personal disposition. We are not all born into Mandela's context and we are not all born with the same longings or capacities. We can just make the best of what is put in front of us.

Our mission represents the greatest meaning we can bring to our path through life. That life path is the intersection of fate and freewill. We carve and sculpt our life path out of the stone we are given through birth and circumstance.

A guide to personal mission: it is simply what gives us the deepest sense of satisfaction. It is dangerous to give this process a moral twist by saying one mission is more noble than another. We bring our 'noble' missions down from lofty moral heights by reminding ourselves the pleasure is ours. I do what really turns me on. You need to do what really turns you on.

A mother or father who decides their mission is to stay at home and devote themselves to bringing up their children can be following their personal mission as much as Mandela followed his.

Mandela had his song.
I have mine. What is yours?

Most missions of any genuine worth (measured by depth of pleasure) do involve serving others, giving pleasure to others. Missions that involve cruelty or oppression do not bring lasting pleasure or happiness to anyone. The idea of a smiling devil, a happy tyrant, a contented serial killer, is good for Hollywood movies because it elicits strong emotions in the viewer – and our own ego desire for vengeance – but doesn't belong to real life.

Real-life villains – apart from never being one hundred percent villainous – are haunted, fearful figures, poisoned by the bile of their own hatred and violence. The pleasure gained from harming others (or the results of harming others) turns back on the perpetrator sooner or later. If we intentionally harm others, displeasure will always outweigh pleasure in the end.

Here are two more examples of the soul at deep play that don't require Mandela-like proportions.

A friend of mine lives in Wales with his wife and six children. They live on the mountainside without much luxury or money

– they have never had a TV. Theirs is the most harmonious family I have ever encountered.

What a work of art!

They have fashioned a life for themselves and their family that is totally congruent with their deepest values.

The other example is my marriage. I take great pride and pleasure in my marriage (so far). Right from the start, right from our wedding ceremony, this is something we have created together, my wife and I. I feel proud of the way we have struggled through the typical challenges that beset most marriages: the sweat and blood of learning to learn in relationship, the journey over the peaks of happiness and through the valleys of disappointment that we have taken together.

We have at times torn up the rules and started again, always searching for the relationship that suits us best; a relationship that is based on our values, our imprint, our truth. Our marriage is an adventure, an exploration, an act of creativity, devotion and persistence.

Relationships, career, and hobbies are all expressions of creativity: they are key to how we fashion our lives. But our creativity can be squeezed and blocked by habit and conformity. Our deepest longings and most authentic impulses are often shrouded in the mist of the norms that surround us and cloak our minds. More will be said about this in chapter 6, The Killjoys.

THE VIRTUOUS SOUL

Virtue sounds like the sort of stuffy noun I used to see declined in my Latin grammar book and which Cicero would use *ad nauseam* in his speeches, usually flanked by two other abstract nouns...

More recently I have grown to love and respect the concept of virtue.

The original Latin meaning of the word refers not only to moral excellence, but any kind of excellence. A virtuous soul, in my book, is one that aspires to the best in everything she does.

What I have just said will hardly seem revolutionary. The difference, however, is that I am relating this pursuit of excellence to pleasure. Soul pleasure is the *end-goal*, not the observance of some moral code. I am saying go for excellence because it will make you feel good – a feel-good that lasts.

Let's explore further this relationship between morality and pleasure, which many will find problematic. How can the virtuous soul bring us pleasure through right action?

I love hearing redemption stories: people who are brave enough to 'sin' and brave enough to mend their ways. In these stories you see and feel the transformation from ego to soul pleasure, the release from the prison of the ego into the open countryside of the soul.

I still remember with pleasure moments at school when I stood up for my friends before the authorities, moments when I dared to do what felt right. I also remember with stabs of remorse the moments when I hurt people out of callousness or vindictiveness. Thirty-five years later and I still feel these things! Soul pleasure lasts. So does soul pain.

Soul pleasure accompanies a feeling of rightness and integrity. I mean here an intuitive, inner feeling of rightness, not an adherence to a deontological code. The virtuous soul gains pleasure not from doing the right thing but from doing what feels right. Doing the right thing suggests an external reference point: following the book. Or even the Book. A feeling of rightness is the product of an internal reference point and does not belong to a truth system 'out there' that has to be followed.

Of course external truth systems become internalized and then to a certain extent feel right because they are familiar. This notion fuels Freud's theory of the super-ego. But truths that are 'introjects' – truths we have swallowed often unconsciously and without reflection – will not necessarily continue to feel right if examined critically.

The deep feeling of rightness I am talking about can come only as a result of conscious, critical reflection and processing. In other words, our individual conscience has to disentangle and individuate from the various group and systemic consciences to which we belong by birth and upbringing.

Foucault said ethics is the ultimate expression of freedom. Virtue is an act of creativity. Doing what feels right is what we choose to make of our lives. If we follow externalized norms and 'do the done thing' without challenge or reflection, there is no creativity and thus, in my mind, no genuine virtue. The pleasure derived will be correspondingly less.

You know you are experiencing a soul pleasure when you feel proud and humble at the same time. There is no sense of victory; you haven't scored a point. You just notice and enjoy the state of wholeness within. You feel more spacious in your subjective world, more compassionate, more peaceful.

The concept of self-worth does not apply here, because there is no acute sense of identity within the soul. An acute sense of identity – this is ME! – belongs more to the ego world. At a soul level the boundaries are not thick, the texture of our consciousness is spacious, not dense.

If you feel proud but not humble, that is an ego pleasure. The pleasure derived from a feeling of moral superiority is not sustainable and will evoke a backlash of some kind. The soul gets no pleasure from comparing her own virtue to the iniquity of others. She is reluctant to judge others.

The pleasure derived from a genuine feeling of having done the right thing is a soul pleasure. The doctor in Haiti is experiencing a soul pleasure – being in the right place at the right time doing what feels right to him. And such a pleasure is available indefinitely: on our deathbed such a recollection can still bring us pleasure.

My personal experience as I have grown older is to be clearer when I have done something 'wrong' or 'right'. My guidance system is primarily physical and emotional. I know I have done something wrong because of a strong tension in my body: a physical and emotional contraction. It is a pain that eats away at me. If I banish it from my conscious mind it will just eat away at my unconscious (or at my body), unbeknown to me. That discomfort does not go away till I have taken action to show remorse. That discomfort will remain somewhere in my system until there is reconciliation. In extreme cases, that sense of guilt and discomfort will even remain in my whole family system. The Biblical concept of the 'sins of the fathers' being transferred to their sons has nothing to do with a vengeful God dispensing justice from above because he feels insulted. If we do something truly atrocious, the wound will lie so deep in our unconscious that others with close bonds to us will be affected. As Freud said, the unconscious of the children knows the unconscious of the parents. This is why people are often so anxious to be forgiven their sins on their deathbed. They seek relief for themselves and those who come after.

When I have said sorry or done what I needed to redress the balance, I immediately feel lighter, a weight is off my shoulders. In extreme cases, the burden may never go away completely, but the discomfort can definitely be ameliorated through 'doing what feels right'. And when I do what feels right, I feel myself walking taller. I don't mean with chest puffed out – that is the body language of an ego pleasure – but standing straight, unburdened, with a 'clear' conscience. I feel clean.

We will explore in more detail in chapter ɪɪ the idea of using the pleasure/pain phenomenon as a compass. I believe that our only, ultimate measure of right and wrong is a refined sensitivity to our own pleasure and pain. The work needed to arrive at such sensitivity is enormous: a lifetime's job, in fact.

"The unexamined life is not worth living," Socrates famously said. If life remains unexamined we will not be able to undergo this conscience-sifting process, and we will be denied some of life's deepest pleasures.

Of course if we wrestle our sense of rightness away from established moral norms, we open ourselves to serious doubts and criticisms: What if your sense of rightness leads you to acts of cruelty? How do you know your sense of rightness is not an ego pleasure in disguise? How can you escape charges of gross subjectivity in your analyses of rightness?

By relating everything to pleasure I am indeed inviting subjectivity. Pleasure and pain are entirely subjective in the sense that you, and only you, can say what gives you pleasure and how much of it. I am saying that pleasure and pain are the most fundamental contours of our inner subjective world and partly define our sense of 'I'.

But the subjectivity I am inviting is not 'gross'. I am inviting a refined and disciplined form of subjectivity.

This refinement comes though 'inner empiricism' which I will explain in more detail later in the book. We need to become scientists of our own internal world.

The hedonism I am suggesting is a path of discipline, not dissolution. To have faith in our sense of rightness, we have to work on ourselves. We need to develop a new level of conscience. This work starts with the painful process of disentangling ourselves from the conscience of the various familial and cultural groups into which we are born and part of.

Until we individuate sufficiently from the various norms that we have swallowed, we cannot possess a trustworthy sense of rightness. There are countless examples of people who have committed atrocities in good conscience – because they feel supported by a certain 'group conscience'.

Even genocide has been committed in good conscience. But always informed by a *group* conscience.

I believe that in the moment of cruelty, and even for as long as the bubble of group conscience holds a person, they might experience some sense of rightness and consequent pleasure. I do not believe that such a pleasure can be lasting or fulfilling. Ghosts will haunt and inflict pain on the perpetrator, and, even worse, those connected to them.

A virtuous soul cannot ignore the pain of others. The deep pleasure of the soul often acquires its depth from a regard for others. An act of intentional harm or cruelty is always an ego pleasure. An ego pleasure occurs when we are so wrapped up in that part of our psyche that either aggrandizes or diminishes ourselves that we cannot really see or feel the 'other'. The other is experienced as an object, not as another subject.

If we truly feel the pain and suffering of the other, we cannot indulge in an act of intentional cruelty because it will no longer bring us any pleasure, only pain. Witnessing the pain of the other will blot out our own petty ego pleasure. The sadist (and we are all

THE DISCIPLINE OF PLEASURE

sadists at some time or other) who looks down at the pain of their victim and gleans some satisfaction from seeing this pain is not 'seeing' the other. Truly seeing the other involves also feeling the other. If we feel the pain of the other, we will stop in our tracks. Their pain will be too painful for us.

Nevertheless, at times we will consciously choose to take an action which we know will cause pain to others, such as walking away from a dysfunctional relationship or making any decision we know will disappoint others. If this decision is coming from the right place in us, the soul, we cannot but feel sadness and compassion for those we hurt. The decision will be conscious, compassionate, and non-vindictive.

Compassion is an essential element in many sources of soul pleasure and, as we learnt in chapter 5a, can liberate us from ego. Deep satisfaction can come from opening one's heart to the suffering of others. I remember feeling despair for the umpteenth time at reading the umpteenth story of tragedy and atrocity in the newspaper. I was on a plane and wept. Then I happened to remember something I had heard from the spiritual pundit Ram Dass. Someone had come to him with a similar predicament: "What do you do when your heart breaks at hearing such tragedies?" He answered that you must just keep letting your heart be broken…

My understanding of this comment is that this breaking of the heart is what is needed for the heart to open up. Only then can deeper, more permanent levels of love and compassion be accessed. And those deeper levels of compassion feel better than a closed heart. More pain may appear initially, but in time so too will the warmth and pleasure of more love and compassion.

One antidote to the subjectivism of the virtuous soul is a kind of inner empiricism (see chapter 7) and individuation. The other antidote is the regular publication of the workings of our conscience. We need the help of friends, mentors, coaches or peer groups. My conscience needs to be thoroughly shaken and rattled by others – though I remain the ultimate judge because only I have access to the subtleties of pleasure and pain that provide the inner compass. Numerous times in my life, through checking my inner state of mind and feelings with others, I have become aware of my blind spots: those parts of me and my history that have not received the full light of disciplined reflection. We need access to people who can challenge us.

To conclude, we have two aspects of the soul: the creative soul and the virtuous soul. Together, and when harnessed properly, these two aspects create the kind of life for which we have longed. And when these longings are fulfilled the result is pleasure: pleasure of the soul.

Soul to Soul

ONE OF THE GREATEST PLEASURES IN LIFE COMES FROM A meeting of souls. The moment when all masks are dropped and we see each other in our purity. The place where life paths cross and destiny is revealed:

I *know* you.

A place beyond power and pretence, beyond strife and competition. A space between beings (and possibly animals) where nothing happens, but everything is electric. A 'zone' is felt.

This is the I-Thou relationship espoused by the existentialist philosopher Martin Buber: a meeting between people when they are at their best and noblest. A meeting where the interior worlds of people are in that moment liberated from the control of the ego and the beauty of humanity can shine through.

In these moments, the soul is highly permeable: Spirit seeps through and adds a sprinkle of fairy dust.
But we are not 'one', we are distinct entities – otherwise we couldn't see each other. Our separateness highlights our sameness, our sameness highlights our separateness.
We see from our heart, we see from our soul. We feel energized and awake, glad to be alive and glad that others are alive with us.

Such meetings can happen in twos and also in groups.

The band of brothers who have been through hell together and survived, the band of sisters who have shared their deepest griefs, the team that has achieved success against all odds.

A group of friends at a dinner party who suddenly find themselves in new territory together.

Disclosure and intimacy, vulnerability and courage.
The vibration changes. The texture of the air in the room intensifies.
Eyes glisten, postures become more alert.
Laughter comes more from the belly, silences have meaning.
Insights follow revelations,
love and respect appear without effort,
like the fragrance of a flower.

A family who finally find each other again after all the heartache and feel the stream of blood-love flowing again between them. The son who feels acknowledged by his father and bows his head in respect, the daughter who feels understood by her mother and cries with relief.

I am not just talking about harmony here. Difference is acknowledged and celebrated. This phenomenon can even appear in situations of extreme conflict.

As in all the deeper forms of pleasure, the interior of individuals has changed. People are experiencing themselves and others from an expanded inner space.

Furthermore, the shared interiority of the couple or group has changed. Some hidden potential of that relationship or network of relationships has been revealed and enjoyed.

I have seen this hundreds of times in groups I have worked with.

The mists of fear and defence dissolve and a new, shared landscape appears. This is the world of the soul in communion with other souls.

Spirit Pleasures

"If you knew yourself for even one moment,
if you could just glimpse your most beautiful face,
maybe you wouldn't slumber so deeply
in that house of clay.
Why not move into your house of joy
and shine into every crevice!
For you are the secret
Treasure-bearer,
and always have been.
Didn't you know?"
   – Rumi

Even the briefest examination of accounts of spiritual and mystical experience will reveal some of the richest, pleasure-laden language that can be found. The superlatives within our pleasure gamut, such as joy, ecstasy, and bliss, tend to be found most often within the spiritual and mystical domains (and glossy magazines, of course). Take this statement by Indian mystic Ramakrishna:

"God is a lake of nectar."

He doesn't say God is wise, or God is just, or God is good. He says God is a lake of nectar! In other words God *tastes* good.

Theresa of Avila asks what greater pleasure there can be than to embrace all creatures in love from one's innermost being, which is connected to God.

Extraordinarily, most hedonist philosophers and thinkers, from Epicurus to modern French philosopher Michel Onfray, either deny or ignore the spiritual realm; they tend to be both materialists and atheists. Imagine being a wine connoisseur and leaving out the Bordeaux region…

Perhaps this reluctance to admit to the possibility of spirit arises from an aversion to superstition and institutionalized religion. Or perhaps they simply haven't had such an experience themselves.

Spirit pleasure is the flower of spiritual experience.
Spiritual experience demands no creed, no dogma, no faith, no theology, no moral code.

We are talking here about what William James called "religious sentiment", or "personal religion", not the membership of a particular religious order (though the two can, and sometimes do, coincide).

James's compatriot Ralph Emerson expresses this eloquently (as one would expect):

" … A sentiment which we call the religious sentiment, and which makes our highest happiness. Wonderful is its power to charm and command. It is a mountain air. It is the embalmer of the world. It makes the sky and hills sublime, and the silent song of the stars is it. It is the beatitude of man. It makes him illimitable… Deep melodies wander through his soul from supreme wisdom."

Sounds suspiciously pleasurable to me…

Despite the ineffability customarily attributed to mystical experience, when mystics do burst forth into words or art to describe their experience, the language is hardly one of gloom and misery… Just read more of Rumi or Theresa of Avila when they describe their mystical experiences. Listen to the songs of Hildegard von Bingen, gaze at the paintings of William Blake that depict the *'unio mystica'*.

These days this distinction between orthodox religion and religious sentiment is usually expressed as the difference between religion and spirituality.

Of course membership of a religious institution can offer a different kind of pleasure: the safety and satisfaction of belonging to a well-defined group. Spirit pleasure though comes from a different source. *The* source, many would say. The source that unites the inner and outer.

So what happens to the 'subject' when spirit pleasure occurs?

An ego pleasure is sought and enjoyed by the ignoble 'I',
a soul pleasure is sought and enjoyed by the noble 'I',
and a spirit pleasure derives from no 'I'.

There is no agency involved in a spirit pleasure. It is not something we can decide to go out and do or get.

Pleasures of the spirit have a transcendent quality that dissolves the sense of 'I'. And that dissolution is essentially pleasurable. If a soul pleasure is about learning and building, a spirit pleasure is more about unlearning and disappearing. It can also be intense and frightening, but there is an unmistakable flavour of joy, contentment, or outright ecstasy.

Spirit pleasures usually involve a union of some kind, a union felt at both a visceral and transcendental level. Spirit pleasures do not occur in the abstract or in fantasy; they are overwhelmingly 'now' and vivid. Although the experience takes us far beyond our personal boundaries, even obliterating the boundaries, it is as if the event permeates to our core, and even leads us to the core of the universe.

I am not saying that mystical experience can be reduced to a feeling of pleasure, but I am saying that pleasure tends to accompany spiritual experience – and that pleasure is probably as good as it gets.

A love-making during which the heavens move, a feeling of profound oneness with nature, a moment of music when listener and listened disappear as two separate forms, an instant or period of contemplative unity when we finally melt into the arms of the universe – these are the kinds of triggers for spirit pleasure.

Jesus is reported to have said that when the outer becomes the inner and the inner becomes the outer, there we will find the kingdom of heaven: a sense of unity. A light goes on in our felt world and that light has an edge of delicious pleasure.

If you are a gentle panpsychist like me, who believes that all matter has some kind of interior, some kind of conscious spark, then being on the inside of yourself is ultimately being on the inside of everything. The whole universe has an interiority that, when felt, is intensely pleasurable. There I feel at home, connected to all. My inner world, my sense of self, expands to include everything on the outside. I no longer feel separate.

Such statements are easy to ridicule, easy to dismiss, but the pleasure behind the statements is harder to dismiss. You can dismiss people's interpretations, but you can't dismiss their depth of pleasure. Sceptics will say that this could be a trick of the mind, a self-delusion. In my language, sceptics are thereby implying that spiritual experience could be a mere ego pleasure in disguise. But how likely is it that 'mere ego pleasures' can be consistently – cross-culture, cross-history – described in terms of rapture, ecstasy and deep contentment?

How 'unscientific' to discount such evidence!

Just creations of the brain, the physicalists will say.

What in our lives is *not* partly a creation of the brain? Our brains enliven an essentially dull universe; our minds enable us to see stars, hear birds, smell flowers. Spiritual experience, like any other experience, is a co-construction: a composite of inner and outer, a reality that is partly out there, partly created within.

William James carries out a marvellous deconstruction of what he calls 'medical materialism', whose apparent mission is to belittle spiritual experience and consign it to mere biology:

"Medical materialism finishes up St Paul by calling his vision on the road to Damascus a discharging lesion of the occipital cortex, he being an epileptic. It snuffs out St Theresa as a hysteric, St Francis as a hereditary degenerate."

These days Postmodern Pete joins hands with the evolutionary biologists and militant atheists and reduces spiritual experience either to a particular cultural trend or a survival-based hardwiring in the DNA.

All of these positions have some truth, but that truth is partial and blatantly discounts the subjective but incontrovertible experience of pleasure. Enveloped as they are in their quest for truth at all costs, such positions conveniently ignore the one part of the whole experience that really matters: the interior, *felt* world.

There is plenty of literature from both Eastern and Western spiritual traditions that charts the different spiritual states, experiences and realizations. From Plotinus to Sri Aurobindo to Ken Wilber, there are people who have devoted their lives to living, sharing and communicating their spiritual path and the joys and struggles that accompany such a path.

However, in none of the spiritual literature and teachings I have been exposed to has the lens of pleasure been used. Indeed most spiritual traditions, like the rest of society, tend to treat pleasure with suspicion. Truth is regarded as the real goal: to find out who we really are and what is our true relationship to the divine. The

Dalai Lama has moved more in the pleasure direction as with his book on happiness, but some might question whether that book is really about spiritual or mystical experience.

In my own experience, spiritual pleasure comes in two categories: uppers and downers, so to speak.

Peaks and valleys. Ascendant and descendent. Equally beautiful but different.

Ascendant is ecstatic: we are uplifted, we are elated, it is as if God (or whatever you want to call her) invades us, plucks us out of our little world and sends us soaring into the sky of being. *Descendent* is cooler and takes us softly to our depths. A vast silent emptiness that enfolds us, laying every thought and desire to rest. Experienced in terms of love, ascendant is *eros*, descendent is *agape*.

Here is an example from the Buddhist archives which points to the descendent:

"One day, in a mood of sublime emptiness, Subhuti was resting underneath a tree when flowers began to fall about him.

'We are praising you for your discourse on emptiness,' the gods whispered to Subhuti.

'But I have not spoken of emptiness,' replied Subhuti.

'You have not spoken of emptiness, we have not heard emptiness,' responded the gods. 'This is the true emptiness.'

The blossoms showered upon Subhuti as rain."

The showering blossoms suggest such beauty and effortless pleasure – combined with a breathtaking vision of reality. It is as if nothing is happening, and yet everything is there. As so often, the spiritual experience or state is accompanied not only by pleasure, but also by a startling insight into the nature of things. As always with spiritual pleasure, the insight is not sought, the pleasure is not sought – it all happens through grace.

To illustrate ascendant spiritual pleasure, I have a story of my own. I was living in Kyoto, Japan. I had been told of a famous Zen garden, perhaps the most famous Zen garden, located at the temple of Ryoanji.

I arrived at the stone garden feeling distracted. I sat down with the other 'tourists' to contemplate the garden from the side (one is not allowed to walk within the garden itself). My mind was thick with thought. I was hardly aware of my surroundings. Gradually, though, the garden before me began to take shape.

At first sight Ryoanji looks like a bunch of rocks dumped in a gravel car park. Yet within minutes tears began to stream down my face. I felt overwhelmed by a wild, benevolent force that began to shake my body. The rocks and gravel suddenly seemed perfect!

The feeling was too much to hold, surrounded by a camera-flashing public, so I left the garden for fear of disturbing others or making a fool of myself. I started running. I will never know quite how it happened, because I never managed to retrace my steps, however hard I tried, but I ended up round the back of the temple precinct where the trees and shrubbery start to slope up the hills that enfold Kyoto in their green lap.

Waves of energy were crashing through my body.

I found myself kneeling down on the grass and when I opened my eyes, I was near a few old graves tucked between the trees. When I saw the graves, the tears flowed again.

I still don't know to whom those graves belonged, but in that moment I felt in the presence of something vast. Almost biblical: the glory of the Lord shone down! I was in awe.

It didn't matter which or whose Lord: just some divine presence. Some ultimate 'Thou'. Then came a message:

"The only true joy is to serve me."

I felt a surge of bliss run through me like an electric shock. Almost painful in its intensity. I then found myself moving up the mountain and as I did so, I started getting visions. I could see things that are usually veiled:

> *My past and my future rolled out before me like a carpet,*
> *all my wisdom and follies, all my dark corners exposed,*
> *all my light magnified. Everything crystal clear.*

And if I pictured someone I knew, I saw the same for them.

Of course there are many possible interpretations to such an experience – psychological, spiritual and even cultural. I am not interested here in looking through a truth lens: what was real or not real? I am interested in applying the pleasure lens.

First and foremost is the power of the spirit dimension: the excitement and intensity of being overwhelmed in this way; the relief, if only briefly, of having all my petty thoughts and concerns swept away by something much bigger than myself. Not only did I feel the joy of humility, I also felt – simultaneously – the majesty of a greater power course through my veins.

The whole event started with an aesthetic experience: gazing at a Zen garden. Spirit pleasures are sometimes just the deepening of a simple pleasure. These are similar in that the sense of an 'I' is minimal:

Where is the sense of 'I' in suddenly hearing a bird sing?

Where is the sense of 'I' in being overwhelmed by something greater than myself?

With simple pleasure, there is no real 'I' present. In spiritual pleasure the 'I' is transformed into something transpersonal.

Zen calls these mystical epiphanies *satoris*.

Zen also says, as do most mystical traditions, that *satoris* are far from being the ultimate goal. They are more like sweets on the way to keep us happy. The ultimate goal is 'enlightenment' – a state of being indicated by *satoris*, but permanent and beyond any particular experience or event. Indeed, beyond space and time in general.

The 'realized' teachers claim this ultimate state is who we really are. Such teachers would probably bristle at having enlightenment described in terms of pleasure and yet their consistent implication is that enlightenment is the jackpot as far as feel-good is concerned: the pearl beyond price.

The purpose of this book is not to debate whether a state of total liberation is possible. Then we would be on the truth trail rather than the pleasure trail. But I do think the pleasure lens is more important than is generally acknowledged in the spiritual world, a world I have inhabited for many years.

The subtext of all spiritual endeavour is the pursuit of happiness. What is the point of devoting ourselves to a spiritual practice if we don't think that somewhere down the line (after death for some) we will be the happier for it? Presumably the enlightened state feels better than the unenlightened state! Why else would Buddha come up with an eight-fold path out of misery and suffering? Why else all the endless hours sweating in the zendo, praying from the pews, and muttering the mantras?

I have only experienced *satoris*; I am definitely unenlightened in that respect – otherwise I might be writing a different book – but the vast majority of people in the world operate in the same murky, unenlightened waters as myself.

At a certain point on my spiritual path the quest for truth became more a hindrance than a help. I lost touch with my own pleasure compass, my own reference point, my own sense of the quality of my life. I was under the spell of an exaggerated 'truth' orientation: *Who am I really? What is the meaning of life? What is the nature of the universe? What is the sound of one hand clapping?*

Such questions have their place, but the answers have to land at some point in a concrete improvement of life: a self-evaluated, incarnated sense of well-being and happiness.

Ultimately, the pleasure lens is a more accurate means of evaluation than proximity to truth. *Is all this spiritual stuff making me happier? Is all this spiritual stuff lessening my suffering?* Furthermore, the pleasure lens keeps us in touch with one of our key roots: the pleasure impulse.

The pleasure lens keeps our feet on the ground.

And if one's pursuit of pleasure is truly disciplined, surely, if there is an ultimate bliss state, one will arrive there in due course? You just have to keep following the yellow-brick road of pleasure… even if at a certain point that means leaving all roads.

The point is that spirit pleasure feels real.
The point is that spirit pleasure is delicious.

When the veil drops and you are standing in a spiritual shower, you are likely to feel joy, you are likely to feel love, you are likely to feel free.

There is far too much evidence, cross-culture, cross-history that humans can experience this pleasure, albeit in many different shades and forms. It would be illogical bordering on the perverse for a hedonist to refrain from exploring this realm.

However, nowhere is the pleasure paradox more pertinent than in relation to pleasures of the spirit: the more you seek, the more you won't find. The more you chase it, the more spirit pleasure will elude you.

That is both the paradox and the challenge.
Spirit pleasure comes with effortless ease and grace.
We cannot will it or manufacture it. Yet we have to work for it.
We have to prepare the soil of our interior world.

To conclude this chapter, here is a tip from poet William Blake on how to keep the spirit pleasure portal open:

Eternity

He who binds to himself a joy
Does the winged life destroy;
But he who kisses the joy as it flies
Lives in eternity's sunrise.

Composite Pleasures

CAN PLEASURES REALLY BE DIVIDED, AS I HAVE DONE, SO neatly and discreetly?

Of course not. As we all know, the map is not the territory.

One event can trigger various (if not all) different pleasures, though one will usually dominate at any particular time. If, as I am saying, the kind of pleasure we have depends on our inner world, the state of the subject, then the pleasure will shift according to our inner states – which can shift swiftly.

If we go back to Ryoanji and use the pleasure map to chart the territory covered during that experience, we see that various kinds of pleasure were involved. First was the simple aesthetic pleasure of the garden (which I missed), then the sweeping pleasure of the spirit, and eventually some soul work making sense of it all.

Plus some ego stuff for good measure.

Because the pleasure impulse is so pervasive and searches every nook and cranny of our being for expression, spirit pleasures can easily be followed by an ego pleasure, especially after the fact:

I had an amazing experience. I am God's chosen one. I have had an epiphany or satori.

See how easily the sense of 'I' can reassert itself and attune to the pleasure impulse from an egoic place? If this egoic hijacking takes place in a big way, much of the spirit and soul pleasure will be lost.

The follow-up to the Ryoanji event is a perfect example of this. I was recounting my story with great pride and enthusiasm to a colleague of mine, an ordained Zen priest of some 20 years. He listened carefully, paused at the end, and said:

"Well, that is a remarkable experience... but it could have happened on the toilet too."

This is of course Zen at its deconstructive best. What was so clever about this comment was that he pricked two bubbles with one barb: both my own ego bubble and any bubble I might create around Ryoanji itself. I am eternally grateful to him for helping me retain the humility I had so enjoyed during the experience itself. However, I do doubt I could have had that specific experience on the toilet; other great epiphanies, perhaps. I think Ryoanji was more than just a random trigger, but the Zen monk said the right thing at the right time.

Similarly, it is easy for a soul pleasure – doing what feels right, for example – to turn into an ego pleasure: *Look at me doing what feels right and look how special I am!*

Only the ego will gain pleasure out of a comparison with others. Self-righteousness is a sign that soul work has been hijacked by the ego.

After the Ryoanji event, my soul got to work in two more ways.

First, with the help of my Zen friend, I reflected on what was to be learnt from this experience: *What does it signify in my life; how does it add to my personal path; how can I make use of it (even if the best use is to let it go)?*

Second, I began to study Zen gardens: visiting them, reading about them, meditating in them, absorbing them.

Spirit states and pleasures are not enough. They need to happen within a soul vehicle on a soul path.

Less distinct perhaps is the composite pleasure that happens when a simple pleasure melts into a spirit pleasure. While we are still hovering round Japan, nowhere is this composite more evident than in Japanese haiku poetry. Here is perhaps the most famous example, by Matsuo Basho, who was heavily influenced by Zen:

Ancient pond...
Frog jumps in
Sound of water.

Much of haiku poetry starts with a simple sensory experience that, through the heightened awareness of the subject, turns into a spiritual experience. On one level, the pond, frog and sound can simply be pleasant to observe, but the poem points to a much deeper existential level.

That split moment captured by the poem is also a doorway to a transcendental experience in which all else disappears except the frog in the water. A union between subject and object occurs where, in Zen terms, the observer becomes the observed. Such an event can send ripples of delight through our being. Such an event can illuminate our view of ourselves in the world. Such an event can turn into poetry that inspires and uplifts people for centuries. Such an event can remain in our mind as a marker of the transpersonal.

Of course these 'haiku moments' do not only arise out of 'nice' perceptions and experiences. One of my other favorite haiku poems from Ozaki Hosai goes like this:

The mis-struck nail
bent its neck.

This image penetrates me like a knife through whipped cream! Or another 'nicer' one of his:

Snow stopped
in the voices of children
the sun shines.

Haiku tends to portray a timeless, ego-less moment when the veil of separation between our inner and outer worlds dissolves and some essential truth is revealed. A simple pleasure is more or less available to anyone, any time. A spiritual pleasure is more elusive, often coming out of the blue. But it is more likely to happen if you have cultivated your heart of awareness.

Hence traditional haiku starts with ordinary sensory experience.

Hence Zen emphasizes the ordinary as the gateway to the extraordinary: chopping the carrots in the kitchen is just as fertile a ground for *satori* as sitting in *zazen* meditation.

This cultivation of the subject is in the case of spiritual pleasure more of an unlearning than a learning, more of a de-conditioning than a conditioning. The famous expression 'Zen Mind, Beginner's Mind' is the goal: to unclutter our minds and meet life from a place of genuine openness and innocence.

Here is an example from a very different field: my elder brother is a Master of Wine and has spent his life dedicated to the oenological cause. One of the things I admire about him is his ability to approach each wine entirely afresh. He adopts a beginner's mind, despite being anchored in years of training. This deep phenomenological stance is reflected in the different levels of appreciation he enjoys: he can be as exultant in the discovery of a cheeky Chilean as he can with a majestic Margaux. He has so fine-tuned his senses that he can bracket out all his judgments and preconceived ideas – and simply be in the moment of tasting with all his being.

Art takes us perhaps even further into this territory that hovers between soul and spirit, as we will explore in more detail in the next chapter. The stone garden at Ryoanji is first and foremost a work of art. Music, paintings, theatre, dance, literature at their best engage our souls and allow spirit to seep through. Simple pleasure is usually involved (colour, sound, shape, movement), but that can deepen and develop into a soul or spirit pleasure.

My hypothesis is that if the soul of the artist is engaged in the act of creation, then the soul of the observer can also be touched. A soul-to-soul meeting then happens much like that described between people in the previous chapter. And it may be that the encounter with the art is so profound that spirit takes over, as at Ryoanji.

Where soul is present, spirit is never far away.

It is vital to feel the different texture of the different pleasures – all of which are related to different inner states and postures. Each pleasure has a different inner texture to which we need to attune and become familiar if our pleasure compass is to be effective. The inner sense of 'I', the subject of soul pleasure, is spacious, humble and compassionate. It is as if the soul has already seen so much, suffered so much for so long, that the shrill arrogance which so typifies the ego is implausible.

However, if we are really to understand and use the pleasure machinery within us, there is no point demonizing ego pleasure – only the ego would do that! The ego is just doing its job, propelled like the other voices in us by the pleasure impulse. There is no psychic surgery available that will cut out the ego and leave just soul and spirit. If our thinking goes in that direction we have already gone astray.

The only sane, healthy attitude towards ego pleasure is to acknowledge the common place from which it comes, compare it with the other forms of pleasure available, and start aiming for deeper and better.

Art and Sport: Meeting of Soul and Spirit

NOWHERE DOES THE GLOVE OF COMPOSITE PLEASURE FIT quite so neatly as with art and sport.

Why do we sigh with aesthetic delight at a Roger Federer backhand?

Why do we come out of the Van Gogh Museum with tears in our eyes?

Why does the song we love on the radio result in goose-bumps?

Why am I lumping these activities and responses together?

Because at their peak, creators and performers access something magical, something that seems to *flow* through them, into expression and on into the perceiver. In my language, spirit seeps through. The breath of the divine streams through the artist and touches the beholder.

Artists, sportspersons and craftsmen and women alike speak of being at times transported, 'in the zone', in a state of *flow*, where actor and activity are one, when effort is no longer needed and everything falls into place. Maybe we can even stretch this category of creativity to include anyone who is master of their craft and produces moments of peak performance. For example, I have seen my wife giving individual coaching, and have marvelled at the artistry she has developed over the years: the dance between her and the client, her subtlety and precision of word and gesture, the delicate silences, timed to perfection…

When I was reading Carol Gilligan's *Birth of Pleasure*, it wasn't just the content, it was also the words – their elegance, their poignancy, their seamlessness. I felt the inspiration and touch of a true adept of thought and word. I could only be moved in this way if she had some access to this state of flow.

The paradox is that on the one hand these moments come as a blessing, as a stroke of grace, but on the other hand such moments tend to happen on the back of intense, long-term discipline and practise. Innate talent requires human endeavour of a certain purity and commitment in order to manifest. Tiger Woods's golf swing looks effortless partly because of all the effort that has been put into it – as he will readily attest.

Moments of peak performance are the intersection of the human and the divine.

The magic is delicately balanced between sweat and grace, between what is within our control and what is outside of it.

We see in these examples the perfect mix of soul and spirit, as described in my pleasure typology. It is as if the world of spirit (we sometimes use the term 'God-given') has created a natural potential which requires the work of a dedicated soul to blossom and re-engage the divine, bringing profound pleasure to all those who bear witness.

Perhaps this explains the pain we feel when we see talent wasted…

The discipline of intent and action that so typifies the work of the soul eventually provides an opening for spirit and moments of grace to occur. In such moments, sense of self is absent in both actor and observer, leaving a trail of delicious absorption and wonder.

We all receive our moments of grace, however small and unheralded.

I attended my first group workshop when I was 17 years old – it was called 'Journey to the Heart'. I was captivated. Three years later I gave my first 'self-development' workshop. It was ridiculous at that age to be facilitating people through a deep personal process: my performance was rough and I was nervous. Yet something in me knew: *I can do this!* It took many more years of trial and error, but today I feel a certain kind of mastery in my craft.

At first glance mastery appears to be a personal achievement, an accumulation of knowledge and experience – all of which is necessary – but in the moments of wonder this all melts into the background. "I" melt into the background. When I am at my best, "I" am hardly there; I feel more like a conduit. I may explain it as, "I know intuitively what to say and do", but this does not represent my inner state accurately – it doesn't feel like *my* knowledge or *my* intuition. I am simply part of a field and have access to the wisdom of that field.

> *True mastery means surrendering to a greater source of wisdom and impulse. If our soul has already done the hard work, we can open up to the power of spirit.*

Another metaphor or even epistemology we can use in relationship to flow and grace is the polytheistic lens employed so beautifully in the book *All Things Shining*, by Dreyfus and Kelly, which draws parallels between Homer and peak human achievements. The book, which offers a sexy antidote to an increasingly secular, materialistic world, is spiritual without reverting to religious orthodoxy or dogma.

When I was young, I was fascinated and enthralled by the stories of Greek gods and heroes. I dreamt of Achilles and longed for Helen, immersing myself in Homer for many years. As the authors explain, the ancient Greeks appeared to attribute 'the magical moments', the moments of peak achievement to the presence of gods and goddesses.

Even today, when my work with groups and teams is in optimal flow, I sometimes feel grey-eyed Athene is with me, other times it is golden Apollo. Then I must hold my tongue and let them speak...

There is a famous passage in 'The Odyssey' (referred to in *All Things Shining*) in which Odysseus and his son Telemachus seem to be receiving unnatural and mysterious support in their endeavour to win back the palace in Ithaca from Penelope's wicked suitors. Telemachus bursts out in amazement at the miraculous phenomena unfolding and his father rebukes him:

"Be silent; curb your thoughts; do not ask questions. This is the work of the Olympians."

In other words: stop thinking, get out of the way, silently bow before the marvel and enjoy!

To open ourselves up to the full gamut of pleasure this life offers us, we need to stretch our minds and attention beyond our own parochial bubble. We need to include the possibility of magic and grace, the source of which is bigger than ourselves and beyond our comprehension. Otherwise we will starve ourselves of certain states and pleasures. This is what, in my mind, so impoverishes the atheist hedonists who take an entirely humanist position.

"There are more things in heaven and earth, Horatio, than are dreamt of in your philosophy..."

In sport and the arts alike, there is of course also another pleasure: that of the sports fan or arts devotee. There are three main kinds of pleasure open to the devotee.

The first is simply the infection of the aesthetic moment: the inspiration and beauty of the expression rubs off on those who witness it. The spirit that has enthused the artist or sportsperson flows into us, the beholder. Even hundreds of years after its conception, we can listen to a piece of music and feel an echo of the ecstasy which first gave birth to the notes.

When 'all things are shining' – and that moment is captured

in some way – there is always the possibility of being touched by those initial rays.

But the pleasure of the devotee is not only aesthetic or spiritual. Could I really enjoy a cover drive of Indian cricketing great Sachin Tendulkar if I hadn't myself played and studied cricket in such depth? I don't believe someone new to cricket would get the same aesthetic satisfaction as an aficionado, as someone who has invested time and energy in understanding a sport. My own soul has also been at work, studying and learning, thereby creating that opening for pleasure. The third kind of pleasure also belongs to the soul realm. It is about loyalty and is found especially in the world of sport. If I am dancing around the room in delight when a British Olympic rowing team scores Gold, my pleasure is not just aesthetic. A bunch of oars splashing around: most of the technical expertise is lost on me! I am jubilant because of my loyalty to Team GB. I belong to a certain social, national or ethnic group. It's not them who have won, but *us*. This brings a feeling of togetherness and solidarity. I will call my brother and share the success with him. There is a 'we-ness' for the devotees, which can open up a different channel of pleasure.

I still derive pleasure from 'my' football team – Liverpool – having won the Champions League in 2005. This loyalty, all those years of commitment (however strange to those who do not belong), have yielded a great potential for pleasure. And pain: I have been suffering at 'our' miserable progress since then...

Of course, this 'we-ness' can also lead to a dangerous crowd mentality and a collective ego can emerge bent on harming others... think of football hooligans or lynch mobs. The slope from soul pleasure to ego pleasure is always slippery.

Yet clearly sport offers a wealth of pleasure that a hedonist cannot ignore. Millions of people around the world are transfixed to sports and sports results every weekend for this very reason.

Sex

THERE IS NO COMPOSITE PLEASURE QUITE AS COMPOSITE, quite as complex, quite as controversial and quite as… pleasurable as sex.

Sex is wonderfully problematic, at times comically so, at times tragically. On the one hand it is one of the ultimate triggers of pleasure, both in the flesh and the fantasy. On the other hand, sex is one of the ultimate triggers of pain in the form of neurosis, abuse, trauma and addiction.

Let's deal with the bad news first.

How did the subject of sex become so loaded? Why did such a basic source of genuine, healthy, life-giving pleasure become so problematic? How did something so beautiful become so ugly in the eyes and bodies of so many?

Sex has endured the hatchet job to end all hatchet jobs.

Sex has itself been abused and raped in the most merciless fashion imaginable.

One could almost say that the more 'civilized' the civilization, the more barbaric its treatment of sex. The best evidence of a collective healthy attitude to sex comes either from pre-agrarian cultures or indigenous cultures that have somehow retained their distance from so-called civilization.

The assault on sex has been institutionalized through almost all religious orthodoxies and every patriarchal society that has ever existed. Religion, politics and consequent jurisdiction have conspired to deflower sex of its innocent pleasure.

There are two aspects to this story of *sexocide*. The first aspect is the association of sex and violence: several thousand years of ubiquitous forced sex perpetrated mostly by men on women, girls and boys. It doesn't require Aristotelean powers of deduction to conclude that as soon as sex is coerced, the experience changes for both parties. For the victim, pleasure is substituted by pain of a horrific nature, both physical and emotional.

However distasteful it may seem, if we are to realize the culture shift towards pleasure that I am suggesting, then we must also understand how the pleasure level of the perpetrator is heavily diminished by any kind of forced sex. The ridiculous belief in circulation in some parts of some societies that violent or forced sex is the most enjoyable has to be overturned. Moral injunctions clearly do not offer enough deterrence on their own.

The best sex of all is without doubt one accompanied by reciprocal love.

What magnifies the basic sensations of simple pleasure connected to the genitals and other erogenous zones and brings a couple into the realm of soul pleasure is simultaneous feelings of love and care. Part of the very joy of sex is the pleasure of the other. When we gaze at our partner while making love and see our love reflected in the eyes of the other, a circle is completed and the pleasure deepens to include the soul.

The second aspect of the sexocide story is the demonization of sex. The iron judgments of church and state, followed up by punishments of steel and fire, have distorted the human view of sex to the point of insanity. In terms of the de-pleasuring of sex, the nadir was reached perhaps in the Middle Ages when it was deemed sinful even to enjoy sex within marriage. Priests were told to give this kind of advice to repentant males:

"Have you coupled with your wife or another woman from behind like dogs? If so then 10 days penance on bread and water."

Then there was also a decree that for a woman to agree to a position other than the 'missionary' was as serious a sin as murder…

Let's not even think about the penance for adultery or homosexuality.

Some of us may laugh at these extremes from the comfort of a relatively liberal environment, but if you dig deeper into the general sexual psyche, you will still find layer upon layer of guilt, shame and insecurity – even among the most liberated.

Listen to the voices of judgment in your head when you hear a woman has more than one lover. Listen to the voices in your head when your teenage son or daughter first makes it clear their sexual preference is different from yours.

The history of sex is so tortured with humiliation, abuse, mutilation and death, one can only gasp in horror. Women have been the main victims as male-dominated societies have tried down the ages to reduce and even stamp out any vestige of female sexuality outside procreation. The loss for men, though less obvious, is also disastrous as it has stripped sex bare of its most precious pleasure: love. Tragically, sex has become intertwined with violence. Venus and Mars never did make a good couple. And were Paris and Helen really the baddies of the show?

Before distancing ourselves from this sad story and appealing to the sexual revolution of the sixties, female emancipation and so on, we must be sure to check out current statistics of coercive sex, which is present in virtually *all* societies. Physical and emotional pain is suffered by millions on a daily basis. Many of the wounds will never heal and will simply be felt by the next generation. Any sexual trauma that is lodged in the unconscious of a mother or father will find its way in some form into the unconscious of their children.

THE DISCIPLINE OF PLEASURE

As writers such as Riane Eisler *(Sacred Pleasure)* have pointed out, the suppression and demonization of sex, and in particular female sexuality, have gone hand in hand with political oppression. Whenever and wherever females have been seen and treated as male property, a kind of sexual slavery has ensued which has mirrored other gross forms of oppression, such as slavery itself. Let us not forget that when the early American colonists were deciding what kind of political and legal status to give the first black slaves from Africa, they chose to adopt the English common law governing the status of married women.

Even today, women's sexuality is closely guarded in many male-dominated societies and behaviour such as adultery is punishable by death, 'honour killings' and so on. Not to mention the massive, international trade in child prostitution. Not to mention genital mutilation. Not to mention the automatic link between war and rape on a scale at which we can only gasp. Not to mention incest, not to mention…

The reason I come out in such a polemic, ejaculatory way when it comes to sex is because there is still a massive reluctance to confront both the atrocities that have been committed and their enduring legacy. Even if they say and think otherwise, most people are still deeply influenced by the historical demonization of sex. As for the (mostly) men in office who continue to commit sexocide, maybe a new category of crime against humanity can be opened at the Hague.

It is as if there is a deep, deep fear of sex and its pleasures.

And an even deeper fear of women enjoying its pleasures.
All downhill from Eve onwards…

Thanks to the 'publication' of sex through the internet and pretty much all forms of media (apart from the Church Gazette), a whole new cluster of performance-related anxieties have evolved around sex. Even those of us who assume we have long since liberated ourselves from the grip of the iron moral judgments, cannot help but occasionally question our potency or sexual attractiveness when bombarded by images of impossibly beautiful bodies indulging in impossibly expert sex.

So, where is the good news?

Well, to start off with, despite such a dismal history, the resilience of love and sex is such that many people have nonetheless found their way to countless moments of passion and pleasure that have left them feeling respected, nourished and glowing.

In its purity, sex can be so simple and so profound. An exquisite exchange of touch, care and love. Partners can *both* enjoy a luscious sharing of pleasure that can soothe our rough existence, elevate us to rapturous heights, and ease us down into the depths of our being. Without the need for any additional resources whatsoever.

Just naked bodies and open hearts.

Sex can include the whole pleasure typology and may even lead us to kinds of pleasure that lie off the map. Here are some of the obvious types:

Ego: Another victory – I am nearly in double figures!
Ego: What a triumph! I have seduced the ultimate alpha male!
Simple: Your lips are so utterly delicious!
Simple: Oh my God that feels amazing right there – oh yes, yes!
Soul: When I look into your eyes, I see an angel. I could never have believed I could love and be loved like this...

Soul: My darling, my soulmate, after all we have gone through…
we always find each other again and meet in desire and love.
Spirit: For a moment I disappeared – we were one!
Spirit: The heavens have moved, we are the stars when we make
love!
(Not that we always actually *say* these things of course.)

Freud viewed sex as the greatest pleasure, but saw sexual pleasure
(all pleasure in fact) primarily in terms of *release*. In other words:
orgasm. Yes, the release of orgasm is one of the greatest simple
pleasures we know, but also available in sex are soul and spirit
pleasures. These have little to do with release and are not restricted
to genital sensation.

Sex is such an intense activity that many different parts of us
get triggered: the terrain of the subject around sex is varied, from
the no-self of spirit to the noble 'I' of the soul to the ignoble 'I'
of the ego.

The ego is inherently unstable and a little desperate: ego will
always try to aggrandize or minimalize itself and ego will always be
looking for scraps from the pleasure table. When it comes to sex,
the ego will swell with pride like Casanova or Delilah, or the ego
will shrivel (sometimes physically!) in self-doubt and self-hatred.

As always the perspective I bring is not a moral one: that ego
pleasure is *bad*. My point is that Casanova's pleasure is not especially pleasurable, especially if someone else gets hurt. As soon as
you view a sexual partner as an *object*, you can forget any soul or
spirit pleasure. Soul pleasure in sex comes from a recognition of
the other: *you and only you*.

If you want more soul pleasure from sex, open your heart.
If you want more spirit pleasure from sex, get over yourself.
Or take a course in Tantra.

So the good news is that sex remains a potential honey pot for the hedonist. And to reach the sweetest honey you may have to dig deep. For those with sexual trauma, the path to pleasure can be long and painful. And we all suffer to some extent from the collective trauma of sexocide committed through the ages.

Even just initiating an inquiry into your sex life in terms of pleasure can be confronting. Everyone thinks about sex, everyone talks about it. At the same time no one *really* thinks it about, no one *really* talks about it. Difficult questions can arise:

Am I really happy with my sex life or lack of it?
Is my partner happy with our sex life?
Do I sometimes have sex when I don't really want to?
Has the passion disappeared?
Am I still attractive to my partner?
Am I a 'good' lover? Is my partner a 'good' lover?
Do I really want to be monogamous?
Have I really explored my sexuality? Do I secretly feel I am missing something?
Do other people have better sex than me?
What do I really like (and not like) in sex?
Am I having sex with someone of the right gender for me?

The road to deeper pleasure often starts with a bold confrontation with reality. We have to dare look at how things actually are before we can change them.

To conclude this chapter, I will return to the somewhat evangelical tone with which I started. It is my belief that true sexual liberation will lead to a more peaceful society. "Make love, not war" is not an empty cliché for me. Contrary to various religious teachings,

I think pleasure should be the primary goal of sex and procreation secondary. The planet is not crying out for extra heads to count... rather it is crying out for love and pleasure.

It is dangerous to take such an analogy too far, but it is interesting to note that within the world of apes, our nearest of kin within the mammal world, the most harmonious are the bonobos. Primatologists speculate that one of the main reasons for this is the high level of sexual activity that is based on equality and not male dominated. In other words, sex is instigated by both sexes. Furthermore, bonobos frequently have more than one partner, indulge freely in sex with their own gender, and are highly creative in their sexual variations.

As one researcher points out, it is as if they have been "following the *Kama Sutra*", unlike "the somewhat boring functional sex of the common chimpanzee".

So it's time to decide once and for all: are you a bonobo or a chimp?

My dearest hope is that future generations will not live in constant fear of forced sex or under the shadow of sexocide, and will simply enjoy sex in the deepest way possible.

The Killjoys

WHERE DOES IT ALL GO WRONG?

Why do we suffer so much?

Is the pleasure impulse not doomed to failure as it bumps up against the reality principle, which suggests an unpredictable, unforgiving world?

Will our own pleasure impulse simply find itself in competition with too many other pleasure impulses flying round the planet?

Is not that first scream of shock as we are wrenched from the warmth, comfort and pleasure of the womb into the cold light of day a sign of things to come?

Buddhism says that the root of suffering is desire.

If the root of suffering is desire and what I am saying is true – that desire for pleasure (what else can we in effect desire?) is hardwired – then life on earth would appear to be a pretty raw deal!

No wonder many people find the idea of a benevolent creator or universe hard to swallow...

I don't know what the purpose of life is, but I am suggesting that refining both our capacity for and path to pleasure gives *a* worthy purpose to life. Is this not the only sane purpose to life? Of course, we are trying to do this anyway due to our innate pleasure impulse. However, we are not very good at it and we come across many enemies to pleasure along the way: the killjoys.

I share with Buddhism the essentially existentialist point of being our own guide in life and talking responsibility for our happiness and salvation. Unlike many forms of Buddhism, I do not believe in these times that renunciation in its various forms is most likely to attract adherents. The postmodern age needs a more pragmatic, utilitarian attitude: we are much too selfish and individualistic for anything else. *What will make me most happy?* is the question. Not *what is the true way?*, not *what is the right way?*, but *what is the most effective way?*

INEVITABLE SHIT

To a certain extent, life just is a bummer.

The slings and arrows of fortune are such that the chance of suffering, some of it on a massive scale, are high (and always have been). Even the 'have-it-all' generation of Westerners to which I belong manages to suffer like hell. We get bored, we get burnt out, we get depressed, we get neurotic, we get paranoid. According to stress research we get thrown deeply off balance just by moving house! Forget war, forget hunger, forget political oppression, we get unhinged by moving from one luxury house to another. All the 'happiness studies' so in vogue at the moment prove that money and comfort beyond a certain minimum limit fail to bring joy and happiness.

We are bound to suffer at some stage in our life, and in our misconceived attempts not to suffer we will often create more suffering, both for ourselves and others. This book will have zero impact on the basic potential for suffering which life pre-supposes. We are fragile physically, we are fragile emotionally. Our

THE DISCIPLINE OF PLEASURE

relationships are fragile, relationships between societies are fragile, and our environment is becoming increasingly fragile. At certain times in our lives, and for some almost continually, we are going to hurt.

However, human beings have two vital soul qualities to assist us through life: *resilience* and *the ability to learn*. The former enables us to endure and go on, and the latter enables us to reduce the suffering and increase the pleasure in our lives. There is inevitable suffering and 'evitable' suffering. Not all suffering is necessary. Our capacity for pleasure can be increased a hundredfold. That is the hope this book offers.

However much you meditate, however much therapy you do,
however positive you try to be,
however much you don't do anything and just get on with life,
inevitable shit will happen.

Bereavement, sickness, disaster, tragedy and heartbreak: they can and will happen. It is ridiculous to think that in the aftermath of a tragedy you can avoid deep pain and sorrow.

"Shit keeps happening even when you are enlightened," my favourite spiritual teacher, Michael Barnett, once said. I think that is a slightly less technical take on the age-old question among Buddhists as to whether the actions of the Buddha still invoke karma once he has become awakened and released from the wheel of Samsara and general human misery.

Another Zen story I have always enjoyed goes like this:

The revered old master of the Zen monastery has just died.

The new master was appointed before he died and lo and behold he is crying his heart out.

"Master, master!" says one of the young tyros. "Why are you crying when you know about the impermanence of life and that death is ultimately an illusion?"

"Yes, I know all that," says the new master, "But the tears just keep coming!"

Even the Zen master can get upset by what life puts on his plate.

But the big shit, the inevitable shit, does have a silver lining:

It is an opportunity for the soul.

The soul can create something meaningful even out of suffering.

The soul can grow out of suffering – and bring deeper levels of fulfilment.

At times all you can do is feel what you feel without any hope or even need for lessening the pain. When our hearts are broken – and I don't just mean in the romantic sense – all we see and feel is pieces of broken heart. We hurt and that is all there is to it.

The only real antidote to that pain is, in the long run, action of the soul: creating a life that at least makes meaning out of what has happened to us.

I once met a man in Palestine who told me his story and showed me his bullet scars and shared the horrors of his imprisonment and torture in an Israeli prison. He didn't exaggerate; he just related facts. He is part of a group of Palestinians who wish to make peace with Israel (at great personal risk within his own community). I asked him once:

"Do the horrors still haunt you?"

"Yes," he said, "I often wake up in the middle of the night. The memories and images come back and I get tense and I sweat. But I am used to this. I just go and lie down somewhere else so I don't disturb my wife. I wait till I calm down, then go back to bed."

What soul work! The way he has transformed his anger and hurt into compassionate action. I shall never forget the quiet dignity and purposefulness of that man.

There are many stories of people throughout history who transform their suffering into something meaningful: the musician who writes a song about his dead child which touches the hearts of millions, the recovered drug-addict who devotes her life to helping others with the same problem, the holocaust survivor, taken to limits that most people will never know, who has shared his insights and wisdom with the world.

Big shit, inevitable suffering, does of course appear to work "against" our happiness. In the long run, however, such circumstances are also a potential doorway to a deeper contentment. Someone who processes and recovers from tragedy will have pleasure resources on the level of soul that others don't have.

There is also something to be said for Nietzche's observation (though like his equally cheerful predecessor Schopenhauer, there may be too much emphasis on pain):

"Did you ever say yes to a pleasure?

Oh my friends, then you also said yes to all pain.

All things are linked, entwined, in love with one another."

Many of the enemies to pleasure refer to unnecessary suffering or unnecessary deprivation of pleasure. I see four main killjoys that affect most of the pleasures within my typology:

1 Desensitization
2 Half-heartedness
3 Shame, guilt and duty
4 Cynicism

Most of us, most of the time, wander around in a trance. Asleep.

When we walk through the garden, how often are we aware of the bird singing, the fragrance of the flowers? When we are on the train. Do we feel the tender waves of love emanating from the mother and baby beside us? When we put our favourite song on the iPod, do we listen with body, heart and soul?

The sensitivity, the love of life and its fruits, the absorption with the wonder of it all – which we had in such abundance as children – become diluted in most adults to the point of watery apathy.

Do we give ourselves a chance to enjoy simple pleasures?

We would rather listen to the endless, repetitive drone of our minds, or we are so deadened that we are no longer even aware of the choice.

An education system with a cognitive bias – so strong that it borders on fundamentalism in its neglect of the whole human being – completes the picture…

The Matrix is right here.
Mass hypnosis.
Wake up! Feel pain, feel pleasure, seek pleasure.
Through attending to pleasure we come alive.

I am in the foothills surrounding Santa Fe.

The mountains lean over me, the desert stretches out before me.

The sun is flashing on the snowy crests, beaming gently on my face.

I usually walk first before jogging to get used to the altitude, but after a while I start jogging, only to realize after a few hundred metres, *No, no! I am not enjoying the sun and the view any more.*

I stop and walk again. Sensitize. Pleasure returns.

At that moment the simple pleasures of the environment are deeper than those of jogging. But to enjoy those pleasures I have to be prepared to break my routine, to be awake to every window of opportunity, every nuance and impulse of my body. Often an intuitive impulse will guide me if I allow it. Intuition for me is somewhere between a sensation and a thought, a feeling in which an insight or message is embedded. In this case: *Stop jogging!*

As I have mentioned, pleasure starts in the body. Pleasure is sensual in origin. As we grow older, many of us, especially in affluent societies in this computer age, lose contact with our bodies. We no longer feel the world in the vivid sensual terms we did as children. Because sex is the most intense form of sensual simple pleasure we know (combined with its 'forbidden fruit' mystique), it gets all the attention. A kiss on the neck, a caress of the genitals, a lick of the nipple, the sight of a naked body in all its glory… such events usually bring such intense pleasure that they rouse us from our stupor.

But the wind can also kiss our neck, the sun can stroke our face, a blossom can fill us with beauty. To enjoy such simple pleasures, our bodies have to be awake – such pleasures are not initially as intense or spectacular as sex. Their subtlety demands a more sensitive receptor.

To develop this, we need to be able to direct our attention away from our mental processes to the felt world. Some cultures still retain this connection to the felt world. The affluent Western culture to which I belong definitely does not, as a whole. As many have pointed out, it is this basic disconnection from our own bodies that leads to our disconnection from, and violent exploitation of, the larger body to which we belong: the planet.

This redirection of attention requires learning and discipline.

There is no shortcut. Or rather, there is a shortcut through drugs, but that doesn't work in the long run: consistent use of drugs results in further desensitization of the body. Neuroscience tells us that addiction deadens pleasure: the pleasure circuitry in our brains becomes weakened. An alcoholic will get less and less pleasure from drinking, a sexaholic will get less and less pleasure from sex. Liking becomes wanting. When the addict indulges, instead of actual pleasure there is merely relief from the wanting.

One could almost define addiction in terms of a disconnect from our body, which will signal its rebellion to this disconnect in the form of aches, pains and sickness. People tend to think a good relationship with the body means doing a lot with it – exercising, stretching, pushing. All such activities may help the health of the body, but they don't necessarily create a more *intimate* relationship with the body. Such a relationship deserves a language of *being* rather than *doing*...

Feeling more the inside of our bodies.
Wearing our bodies with more sensitivity, as we would an expensive dress.
Paying attention to the simple events: breathing, moving, resting.
Attuning to the currents and energies pulsing through the different channels of our body.
Softening the edges of our bodies, allowing them to become porous and absorb our surroundings.

In general, for all forms of pleasure, a strong sense of the 'here and now', a kind of relaxed alertness, is essential – and that awareness is best anchored in the body. There are a hundred things every day that can give us goose bumps of pleasure, but we have to be awake or we will miss them.

We have to be prepared to stop!

To rip up the agenda we have set for ourselves.

Stop in the middle of a walk to smell the flower, stop our train of thoughts to talk to a stranger on the train, stop our work when we hear a particular song. We have to be able to break our own rules, to transgress our routines.

HALF-HEARTEDNESS

There are two main reasons children enjoy themselves so easily:

1 They have no shame about pleasure.

2 They don't think about pleasure, they just commit themselves wholeheartedly to whatever they are doing. And then to the next thing, and then to the next…

There is no mystique to pleasure, especially simple pleasure. All it needs is our total attention and absorption. Pleasure is a side effect of this totality.

But this is the age of multi-tasking, of juggling a hundred things at the same time, of planning our next task while we are still busy with this one.

Just try washing your car with total attention: feel your body moving, feel the warm water, and see the car shining. Pleasure comes.

When you are out for a walk, feel your feet hitting the earth. Let yourself be dazzled by the violent green of the trees, let the birdsong penetrate your world. Pleasure comes.

If you do something, do it totally; if you decide to be somewhere, be there totally.

Rule number one: Be Total!

Rule number two: Be Total!

Rule number three: Be Total!

Unfortunately the mass hypnosis goes beyond mere desensitization of our pleasure receptors to actual corruption of the sensors.
Not only do we lose some of our capacity for joy, but the little that
remains is corroded by the well-meaning but ultimately pernicious
norms that surround us, particularly through guilt and shame.

A traditional explanation of the difference between shame and
guilt is that shame is a public feeling, guilt a private feeling. Both
involve feeling bad and remorseful, but one occurs because we have
been seen or found out, and the other occurs because we have done
something that has gone against our conscience.

A more contemporary differentiation between shame and guilt
is that the former pertains more to identity, the latter to action.
We feel ashamed about who we are and we feel guilty about what
we do. Whichever interpretation we make, both are major killjoys.

One of the reasons small children seem to find it so easy to
experience simple joy is because they are barely affected by either
of these secondary emotions. As they get older, one sees the ten-
tacles of social and familial conditioning slowly gaining a grip on
their lives. Adults will usually only experience the same absence
of shame and guilt under the influence of 'looseners' such as alcohol or drugs.

My young son and I are in the car on our sombre way to school
on a wet, grey Monday. I ask him if he remembers how the old
nursery rhyme goes, "Rain, rain, go away..." His face lights up and
he begins to sing with gusto. Before we know it, the car is rock-
ing with a rousing, giggle-ridden chorus as I join the fun. Simple
pleasure. My son, unlike his elder brothers and sisters, has not
reached the stage of self-consciousness where such a song might

evoke shame, and his company, as often, gives me the excuse to abandon myself.

I am not saying that group norms are never appropriate or that we don't in some way need group norms to feel safe and therefore avoid pain. I am not suggesting we should, or can, go back to a childlike state free of inhibition, but I am suggesting that if we wish to bring more pleasure into our lives, we must be prepared to take risks and break certain social and family norms. In my work I often refer to the 'family religion': the web of semi-conscious, unspoken codes and rules that knit the family culture together.

When unprocessed, when blindly followed, this family religion is a killjoy. Through following our family religion, we may avoid the temporary discomfort that can accompany change, but we limit our capacity for joy. Paradoxically, it is through breaking certain rules and norms that we can return to some kind of personal innocence.

Once, while working with a group of managers, I asked them to relate a recent incident in which they had experienced a strong emotion. One woman described watching a swimming competition; she said how much she had enjoyed seeing all these muscular male bodies and then how her pleasure had been curtailed by subsequent pangs of guilt, for she was a married woman. This, just from looking!

This is pseudo-guilt. She didn't do anything wrong; the event triggered a set of truth-and-norms that comes out of the cultural worldview with which she has grown up. This semi-conscious web of truth-and-norms is the product of 'introjects': truths we have swallowed that lie undigested in our system. (Freud's superego, more or less).

Genuine guilt occurs when we have really done something wrong, as defined by our own individuated conscience. Such wrongdoing hits us painfully at a soul level and can only be redeemed on a soul level – through doing what feels right: apologizing, compensating, reconciling or whatever is appropriate to the deed. When we have done something wrong, like Orestes we will be tormented by the Furies until we have atoned. If we are not aware of our misdeeds, the Furies will find us sooner or later and slap us in the face.

Feelings of genuine guilt will lead us out of suffering through right action; feelings of pseudo-guilt will only serve to hinder pleasure. Genuine guilt is specific and acute. Pseudo-guilt is vague, general and chronic, arising as it does from all the truths-and-norms we have inherited. The only way to tell the difference between these two kinds of guilt is through working on ourselves and disentangling from the web of truth-and-norms we have unwittingly swallowed.

We have to be able to break our own rules. These rules and norms are of course an internalization of the rules and norms around us. In that sense we may also need to transgress and break the rules and norms of our environment to find deeper pleasure. This outer transgression is not however aimed at anyone else and our pleasure is not in any way dependent on the pain and discomfort of others – that would be an ego pleasure.

The woman who felt guilt at enjoying sexy male bodies has to disentangle herself from the conviction that a married woman is not allowed to feel attracted to another man. (What she *does* with that attraction is another matter.)

Like guilt, shame eats into the nerves of our self-worth and paralyses our capacity for pleasure. An example is someone who doesn't dare to reveal their naked body and cannot surrender to the full river of sex because the banks of trust needed to contain the experience have been eroded by shame.

All deep forms of pleasure require in the moment of consummation a *yes* to ourselves and a *yes* to life. Shame is a *no* to ourselves and a *no* to life. Liberation from shame requires hard work and courage. In order to be healed, our naked body will have to be exposed. In order to be loved, we must show the wounds of our un-lovedness and risk healing.

Connected to guilt and the truth-and-norms mindset is the duty culture. Flemish Belgium (where I live) is an absolute master killjoy in this respect. A blind, unconscious sense of duty has all but strangled any natural and spontaneous *joie de vivre* that may have existed in this culture. Mercilessly! The pleasure impulse is still at work here because doing one's duty brings a certain pleasure, or rather avoids a certain pain, but it is often invoked in opposition to pleasure as such:

"Oh, it's fine for you to go and have your fun while I do all the work at home!"

"What would happen if everyone just did what they wanted, tell me that?"

"Yes, but if I don't take responsibility, who will?"

This is Masochist Meg at her best. That nagging voice, sometimes externalized but often inside our own head, which puts duty inexorably before pleasure. The main message of Masochist Meg is that life is something to be endured not enjoyed. Masochist Meg is task-focused, relentless, and scornful of spontaneity, creativity and joy. Of course there is some satisfaction to be gained from doing our list of chores at the weekend and ticking off all our to-do's, but how often do we actually stop and ask ourselves: *am I happy living like this? Is this really how I want to spend my weekend?*

If you want to deaden your life to any depth of pleasure, then keep blindly doing your duty... do the right thing in the eyes of society and your family religion – or any other religion. Be a good martyr to the cause of your cultural upbringing.

> GIVING *is one of the greatest soul pleasures in life.*
> *The soul loves to give, loves to serve, revels in the pleasure of others.*
> *Nothing kills the joy of giving quite like duty and obligation.*
> *Giving only gives joy (in both directions) if it comes from the heart, if it comes as an expression of our creativity in life.*

Immanuel Kant famously said: "Acts of altruism that make the actor feel good are undeserving of praise."

I revere Kant deeply, but this is absurd! Only a robot could be expected to give without pleasure. Why on earth shouldn't giving be a pleasure win-win?

I have been involved in setting up a co-operative of commercial companies that give money and human resources to NGOs and good causes. At the heart of our vision is the pleasure of giving, the involvement of the giver, the meaning such acts can bring to all parties. Social duty and moral imperatives belong to an older, different way of thinking that is an archetypal killjoy!

Yes, sometimes we need a push to break through the crustiness of our ego and liberate our soul energy for giving – but that push is the push of greater pleasure, the urgings of a virtuous soul wanting to create a meaningful life, not some morbid need to reduce the suffering of others by adding to our own!

There is a cost of course to breaking the rules and norms.

As my wife and I have found out, as soon as your marriage takes an alternative, non-conformist route, the truth-and-norms vultures will start circling, waiting to feed on the corpses of the friendships they have discarded at the drop of a hat...

THE DISCIPLINE OF PLEASURE

Most people prefer to break the rules in secret and feel guilty in secret. At least then they don't risk rejection.

As my colleagues and I have found out, working with change is dangerous. As soon as you challenge the status quo of an organization or a particular segment of society, you are opening yourself up to the ego pleasures of others who like nothing better than the sight of a naked, out-stretched neck.

From gossip to ostracism, there are alas many weapons that can be used to generate ego pleasure. This is the world of ego pleasure: unhappy people gleaning some kind of satisfaction from trying to make others unhappy.

But that is also a chance for the soul to grow in courage and conviction. That is the chance for the soul to declare and live by its own values.

Sometimes the cost of breaking the rules may be too much.

Back in Palestine, where I was consulting for an NGO committed to the peace process, a young Palestinian colleague of mine was telling me that he had to get married to one of his cousins. It was quite clear his heart wasn't in this marriage and he was unhappy. In a different socio-political context I can imagine myself advising someone to follow their heart in this kind of situation, but I realized that the cost for him of breaking the norms and disobeying his family was enormous. Apart from the strength of the cultural norms themselves, the political oppression to which his community was, and is, exposed only served to increase the need for solidarity and collective social identity.

Sometimes the pleasure and pain scales are so weighted that the safer course is better.

When highly orthodox truths-and-norms are involved, the stakes are raised considerably: the rules to be broken may stem from a religion, for example, where the rulebook is seen as dictated by God and therefore exists as a non-negotiable external truth. Most forms of fundamentalism operate from this extreme external reference point – almost the opposite of mine, the subjective knowing. However, the pressure of such an explicitly externalized truth-and-norms system can be such that the anticipated pain associated with not conforming will bring more suffering than pleasure – especially if it is done abruptly and without a new context in which the rule-breaker can be held.

Many women, homosexuals and other historically marginalized and oppressed groups have been killed for their rightful pursuit of pleasure in societies where the truth-and-norms are stringent. If disengaging from the truths-and-norms of our heritage continuously brings more pain than pleasure, more fear than relief, then it might be better to go back into the fold and enjoy the sense of security and belonging.

If you belong to a community that is exposed to extreme adversity – persecution, war, occupation, natural disasters and so on – the pleasure of solidarity derived from belonging can be intense and even lifesaving.

Conforming to group norms, wearing a veil, curtailing our individual freedom, may be exactly what is needed at a certain point in our life in order to feel safe or happy.

Ultimately, however, some pleasures will only become available to us if we individuate sufficiently. When and how we individuate will depend on our context and stage of development.

This is why it is so important we stay in touch with our subjective knowing: an emphasis on individuation as I am advocating can also become a truth disembodied from our inner world of happiness and pain.

All we can do is keep evaluating our lives, assessing our

happiness, realizing where a pleasure-informed choice has become a pleasure-killing habit. There are no rules as to what gives pleasure and what exact direction in our lives will yield the most pleasure, just an inner barometer that tells us how happy we actually are. This barometer will be explored in more depth in chapter 10.

CYNICISM

Cynicism acts as a killjoy at all levels of pleasure – simple, soul and spirit. It is no coincidence that the Cynic school of philosophy arose partly in opposition to the Epicureans. The cynical voice in us brings a certain satisfaction, a subtle ego pleasure of superiority: *I can see through the illusions of others and apprehend the real state of human life.*

Cynicism is the easy way out of life.

Cynicism gives the perfect excuse not to attempt change, the perfect excuse not to take risks.

The cynical voice enables us to remain snugly in our miserable comfort zone.

The origin and fuel behind cynicism is pathological and lies in disappointment, in a hope for happiness that was dashed long ago. Underneath cynicism is unprocessed pain, a lost innocence. Somewhere in the course of events a *yes* to life has turned into a *no*.

It is the voice of doubt within us, the voice of sabotage, the voice of scorn.

A postmodern society, understandably weary of grand truths, understandably disappointed by endless wars and hypocrisy, unwilling to believe in anything remotely non-material, has adopted the mantle of cynicism with effortless ease.

Cynicism is an essential part of Postmodern Pete's armoury. It defends him against change and offers him the pale pleasure of security. First, Postmodern Pete will deny the difference between ego and soul pleasure:

"How can you really know the difference between ego and soul?"

"How do you know this subjective knowing is not just another social construct? How do you know that your conscious sense of pleasure and pain is not undermined and influenced by unconscious forces?"

Postmodern Pete will tend to claim that the very notion of soul and spirit pleasures are, like everything else, constructs of ego or superego.

Postmodern Pete is inside most of us in the developed world. He has become a cultural introject firmly embedded in self and society. His cynicism is ready to undermine any castles of hope we might build. All pleasures will be questioned as to their authenticity and integrity, dragged through a biased scrutiny that will destroy every last grain of our well-being. Well, not quite every last grain because the pleasure impulse is still at work behind the cynicism, bringing a certain morbid pleasure – at our own expense!

The world of spirit is treated with even more scorn by Postmodern Pete, reeking as it does of supernaturalism and meta-narrative. The recent growth of secularism, at times militant in nature, has managed largely to throw the spiritual baby out with the religious bathwater. By lumping spiritual experience and religious dogma together, a whole domain of both personal development and pleasure is becoming excluded from the average map.

Traditional forms of psychoanalysis also question the authenticity of spiritual experience. Freud famously reduced the 'oceanic' feeling so sought after in many Eastern forms of spirituality to a longing for the womb and inability to cope with separation and adulthood, thereby implying that spiritual pleasure is in some way pathological and inauthentic. All pleasures can of course be analysed, pathologized, deconstructed and generally shredded, including the pleasure derived by those who do the shredding. Once again this is an example of the truth perspective at work rather than the pleasure perspective.

For the record, I think Freud is right that spiritual pleasures start with the feeling of unity experienced between baby and mother, but that doesn't mean that spiritual pleasures merely revert to that state. The adult form of unity is self-conscious and integrative. *Trans*cendent is not the same as *pre*scendent.

My form of hedonism deals with postmodern cynicism as follows: if a pleasure is 'inauthentic', it is an ego pleasure rather than one of the deeper pleasures. If we are rigorous in our pleasure metrics, the truth will out. If a so-called spirit pleasure is an ego pleasure in disguise, then it won't yield much pleasure and will accordingly be dropped. As for the 'truth' of the situation, does it really matter? Was Subhuti actually making love to his mother under the tree? Were my tears at Ryoanji a subtle form of sublimation? We will never receive definitive answers to these questions, but we do experience, in a very concrete way, different degrees of pleasure in our inner landscape.

In dealing with pleasure in general, we must avoid two forms of reductionism: reduction to the unconscious and reduction to a social construct. These two forms will eat away at our pleasure and in our own minds we will become very clever, very sophisticated and... not very happy.

Inner Empiricism

"When I enter most intimately into what I call myself, I always stumble on some particular perception or other, of heat or cold, or light or shade, love or hatred, pain or pleasure. I never catch myself…"
– John Hume

Empiricism considers *experience* the cornerstone of reality.

Life is made up of a series of perceptions and impressions: a continuous reel of events appearing on the radar of our consciousness.

Pleasure and pain are one of the key ways in which the impact of these events is registered.

In its most primitive form, the pleasure apparatus works as follows:

Event/stimulus – sensation: nice/not nice.

There appears to be an inside and an outside to our experience of life.

On the outside we perceive a world of colour, texture, smell, sound and flavour. *On the inside* we perceive a world of emotion, thought, image, and imagination.

Traditional empiricism emphasizes the exterior world and creates an epistemology (theory of knowledge) around sensory experience. Through adopting traditional empiricism as its fundamental method, science has brought us within the past four hundred years an astonishing array of revolutionary technology that has transformed our lives. On the outside anyway.

However, traditional empiricism has not always been kind to perception that is turned inwards. Indeed, most scientists regard the inner world of feeling, imagination and intuition more as an obstacle to true knowledge than an aid.

You could almost say that the inner world has been oppressed and an inner kind of knowing subjugated by the age of reason. This probably had to happen to help us out of the Dark Ages with its superstition and blind faith… but there needs to arise a new epistemology that honors equally inner and outer sources of information.

The almost ludicrous climax to this subjugation of the inner world occurred within psychology as *behaviourism*: the inner world can't be observed with the senses, can't be measured, can't be perceived as object – so off with its head! Let's delete half of our experience of life!

Yet the path of perception does without doubt point inwards as well as outwards. In practice we take our inner perceptions just as seriously as our outer perceptions. Is a feeling of joy any less real than the sighting of a bird?

As far as pleasure and pain are concerned, we must rely on our inner felt world. It doesn't matter how much you analyze a wound under a microscope – the experiment will not show you how the pain feels on the inside!

We need a form of 'inner empiricism' that demands the same attention and diligence as traditional empiricism. We need to develop an inner eye, an inner organ of perception that is as sensitive as the microscope.

I close my eyes.
I notice a tingling in my fingers, a heaviness in my eyelids.

THE DISCIPLINE OF PLEASURE

I notice my breath is a little short on the in, as if I don't want to breathe the whole world in today.

I notice a wispy ache around my chest, a residual vulnerability from a conversation this morning with my wife. If exaggerated that vulnerability would lead to warm tears.

I notice a thought about what I will do with my son this afternoon. I notice myself following that thought, developing that thought and options emerging.

I notice a ripple of excitement at the thought of hiking.

I notice the heaviness of the eyelids turning into a slight ache above the eyes.

One of the reasons the inner world has been devalued is because it cannot be viewed in the same objective way as the outside world. Which organ of perception picks up on such internal events as emotion, pain, pleasure, intuition? How do you know you have a 'gut feeling'? Can you observe it? Smell it? Touch it?

The poverty of language to describe the inner world is symptomatic of its devaluation. If we look at the descriptions of inner events listed above, it seems there is little option but to use metaphor: are eyelids really heavy? Do they really weigh more when we are tired? Does excitement really take the form of a ripple? Is there a mini-wave flowing through my system? We borrow words from the outside perceptual world and plant them in our inner landscape.

We say "look inside yourself" or "look deep inside your heart". I am no anatomist but presumably there is no inner eye with a pupil and a retina.

We use the word 'feel' to cover just about everything. We feel angry, we feel ashamed, we feel an ache, we feel inadequate. The language of interior perception is poor. And yet our interiority is experienced as being just as real as the exterior world. If we are honest with ourselves, are we not just as sure of the feeling of jealousy as we are of the greenness of the trees?

The other reason the inner world becomes devalued is because the inner world is interpreted as well as observed. A society that gives increasing value to objective science as the yardstick of reality gives short shrift to such subjective phenomena.

The inner world is by definition subjective. Look at the meaning I attribute to the ache in my chest. The inner world demands a different process of perception and a different epistemology – but with the same thoroughness and attention to detail.

Let us look further how interpretation and meaning-making happen in relation to our internal world. We have to decode and uncover the events of our inner world as well as observe.

As I sit down to meditate one morning, I notice a voice of anger in my head, a pang of resentment, a stinging feeling of injustice in regard to a certain group of people in my life.

This voice of resentment has surfaced many times in my interior world.

Before I know it, I have followed this voice into predictable patterns of blame and recrimination, patterns that are an all too familiar part of my inner landscape.

When I look underneath that voice of recrimination, I feel hurt, I feel pain. I attend to that pain, giving it a place. The anger soon softens into sorrow. The voices of recrimination cease and are replaced by a feeling of vulnerability that, if unleashed, disperses through my body, bringing an entirely different texture to my inner world.

From that place of vulnerability, when I imagine those who have wronged me, my picture of them is milder. I haven't abandoned

THE DISCIPLINE OF PLEASURE

some of my views but I feel more compassionate, towards both myself and them. And I suffer less.

This is inner empiricism at work.

To use yet more vocabulary borrowed from outside, our inner world is like a continuous movie that rarely stops – except perhaps during dreamless sleep or advanced states of contemplation.

Movies are there to be watched and interpreted and the inner movie is no exception. A certain amount of detective work is needed, a certain exploration of hermeneutics, to uncover the movie's symbols and secrets: what is underneath the inner sensation or feeling?

Inner empiricism is the discipline of observing and giving meaning to the movie. There are two reasons I believe inner empiricism to be important:

1 Our sensitivity to pleasure is heightened. The more aware we are of our inner landscape, the more pleasure we can feel. Everything becomes more vivid. We feel more connected to our bodies, we feel a more intimate relationship to ourselves. This is home.

2 As we shall see in the next chapter, we need a trained inner monitor in order to navigate life and make decisions. This is how we can feel right and wrong, this is how we can intuit the validity of new directions in our life.

Inner empiricism acts as a counter-balance to an excessive dependence on external truths and norms to guide both our actions and what we think brings us happiness. Historically we have always been told how to behave and what should make us happy.

The truth-and-norms perspective will always draw us outside our own reference point: the norms, the rules, the 'done thing'. It is more about what we *should* feel than what we *do* feel.

Philosopher Ken Wilber talks in a similar vein of a 'broad empiricism' that includes the inner screen of mental, emotional and spiritual data. But to become familiar with this inner screen takes practice and discipline, just as outer empiricism demands. How many times have I asked someone in a workshop what he or she is feeling and received this kind of answer:

"Er, um, nothing much... I don't know really."

Someone who practises inner empiricism will always be connected to what they are feeling on the inside, even if they can't always put it into words. As I always tell people: our inner landscape has weather, just like the outside world. How often do you wake up in the morning and find there is no weather outside?

We need to start mapping our inner territory and becoming familiar with every contour, every weather fluctuation, every movement of the seas. From inner sensation to emotion to imagination to dreams to empty stillness – welcome to the inner world and make yourself at home.

I like John Hume's expression "enter intimately". I often ask people in seminars to "become intimate" with themselves. Though this injunction is sometimes humorously interpreted as a reference to other more obvious forms of pleasure, what I mean is that we get to know our inner territory in the same way as we know every nook and cranny of our house and garden.

There is one big difference between the inner landscape and our physical home and its surroundings: the inner landscape grows as our awareness grows. It can never be fully known – that is part of the adventure of growing our own soul. New vistas will always open up to our surprise and pleasure. And sometimes, temporarily, to our horror.

Inner empiricism is the foundation of all contemplative practice and can be found in some form or other in most spiritual traditions. The goal of meditation is not usually to interpret inner phenomena, but to strengthen the observer or witness. Meditation is awareness folding back on itself. (Perhaps this observer is the elusive 'self' Hume is seeking). The idea is to remain in a state of "choiceless awareness", as J. Krishnamurti put it.

My experience, however, is that the more the observer is strengthened, the greater our capacity to interpret what is observed when necessary. And interpretation is necessary if we are to unblock our pleasure pipes. Pure observation is not enough.

That said, the deeper we go with our inner empiricism, the deeper we go into meditation… the deeper we go in the very act of experiencing of life… and the closer we come to what is called *non-dual awareness.*

Then all is one, there are no two empirical directions.

What is the difference between perceiving a tickling sensation in our leg and the sound of a car outside?

It feels like everything is inside and outside at the same time. The car is passing through our belly. The tickling sensation feels as much 'out there' as the car. It feels like we are on the inside and the outside simultaneously.

Out of that non-dual awareness can arise all sorts of spiritual delights. As we saw in the chapter on spirit pleasure, a new box of chocolates is opened…

Deepest Voice

"As long as a man does not take his responsibility he has doubts and the possibility to withdraw, and his acting is not effective. For all creativity there is an elementary truth: as soon as a man definitely commits himself destiny moves as well. All manner of things that wouldn't have happened otherwise comes to his aid. A veritable stream of happenings follows his decision and furthers it by all kinds of happenstances, meetings and material blessing of which no one could have thought of before they could have helped him on his way. Whatever you believe or think you can do, begin with it. Because you doing works magic, beauty and strength."

– Goethe

I had just returned from Australia via Nepal to a rainy, cold England. My heart was broken and bits of it scattered over the bush I had grown to love. I couldn't go back for visa reasons and although a voice in me desperately wanted to return, I noticed I took no action to do so. I just waited. My feet didn't move.

After some weeks of this, a close Australian friend called me out of the blue from Japan.

"Why don't you come here?" he suggested.

"Okay!" I said. Something told me this was the right place to go – though I didn't know why. I had never planned to go to Japan.

I learnt my first Japanese word in the plane and I had only a couple of hundred pounds on me.

As soon as I was there, something clicked in me: this was it!

A whole life opened up for me, almost immediately. The universe co-operated. Work, money, Zen, beautiful women, friends, the essence of Japanese culture – it all just came to me. I felt rich on every level. And I fashioned what was given to me; I created a good life for myself.

My soul purred.

Three years later, I felt the wind changing again.

I knew I was going to leave. I felt the breeze of change on my face. My soul had stopped purring; what I had created didn't fulfil me any more. The work especially felt increasingly meaningless. I slowly wrapped things up and packed my bags.

My deepest voice had spoken again.

When I returned to Europe a whole other life opened up for me – none of which I had planned, or even dreamed. A new career, a new family, a new home…

At key moments in my life my deepest voice has never failed me.

Not that my deepest voice always signifies movement and change.

One of the biggest decisions in my life was not to follow my heart away from my wife. However much my heart longed for the other woman I had fallen in love with, my feet simply didn't move.

Despite the great pain this caused, and despite my broken heart, I know the decision was right.

In my experience, deepest voice is beyond both mind and heart. Inside our heads there is a cacophony of voices, all competing for our attention and obedience:

Follow me! Do this! Say that!

Somewhere among all these voices is the 'right' voice, the voice that will lead us in the right direction, the voice that brings in the long run most pleasure and least pain, not only for ourselves but also for others.

I call this voice the 'deepest voice'. I first heard this expression from Michael Barnett, my teacher and mentor of many years. It is similar to the Zen concept of 'right action'. I like the expression because it implies that the best we can ever do is find the voice that is the deepest amongst those present. This does not imply deepest in any ultimate sense, just the best we can do with what is on offer.

Gut feeling, inner voice, intuition, maybe even the 'daimon' of Socrates: these are all different expressions for deepest voice. But do we have the capacity to hear this voice and do we have the courage to follow it?

Deepest voice starts with inner empiricism.

We need to become familiar with all the different voices inside us and their different colours and vibrations. Then we learn to identify that voice which will guide us out of the swamp of ego and superego. Ego voices will tend to come from a place of contraction, a place of fear. The ego will want either to enhance or diminish itself. Superego voices are the voices of society, the voices of our parents, the voices of our religion, the voices that are the product of all the truths-and-norms we have swallowed but not properly digested.

I am not saying that deepest voice has an ultimate validity that can be ratified objectively by external sources. Deepest voice is the opposite of following an established behavioural code. Deepest voice is only ultimate within our own universe of voices: deeper than our ego, deeper than the truths-and-norms we have imbibed. Deepest voice does not arise in reaction to external norms, and it may or may not be congruent with those norms. Deepest voice is simply a more profound place within ourselves from which decisions are made.

Our deepest voice, which I believe to be the voice of our soul, is not interested in magnifying or diminishing us. It is not interested in magnifying or diminishing others. It seeks only what is right in each situation. My deepest voice has never failed me (though I have sometimes failed it) – even when it has meant losing out on money, losing out on status, losing out on popularity, losing out on support from my environment. These losses have always been short term. My ego voice, my truths-and-norms voice, has consistently failed me, even if it brought some initial gain.

When I look around me at some of the crazy, ludicrous, horrific decisions that create untold unnecessary suffering in the world, I weep from pain and frustration: decisions made by too many people with too much power having too little contact with their deepest voice. Would investors really have made all those insane decisions that triggered the financial crisis of 2008 if they had a little more sense of inner discernment? Would some of the decisions to declare meaningless wars have been taken if the decision-makers had learnt to differentiate between their ego and their deepest voice?

There are (at least) two great challenges to this concept of a deepest voice.

First, isn't it selfish to follow your deepest voice? (The same challenge to hedonism in general.)

Second, how do you *know* it is your deepest voice, if there is such a thing?

Wouldn't Saddam Hussein have said he was following his deepest voice when he invaded Kuwait?

Selfishness implies an absence of regard for others and our environment, an inability to see beyond our own concerns. My experience of deepest voice is that it is the voice most connected to the actual context of the decision, including the concerns of others. Deepest voice is the voice most connected to the complex web of systems to which we belong. My deepest voice has often led me, for example, to do things that appear to benefit my environment more than myself. My deepest voice is the one best attuned to the wisdom of any field (context) in which I find myself. It is the ego voice that is selfish – in other words a voice that can't see outside its own bubble of reality.

I remember many moments with my stepchildren when I just wanted to escape, give up, free myself from what became an intolerable situation at home. At a key moment when things were at their worst, I had a conversation with a friend whom I trusted. He said, in a very simple way, that I just had to keep my heart open to the child in question and see it through. As soon as he said this, a bell rang inside me: I knew he was right. A deeper voice was awakened in me: I had to find a way to accept the situation, I had to find a way to reconcile myself with what had been put on my plate. No matter how unfair it all seemed, no matter how many insults and other kinds of hurt I had to endure, my heart had to stay in some way open.

I remember running a leadership training once where someone took a secret action behind the scenes to 'help' a colleague in the group. This particular colleague felt utterly betrayed and the incident caused a huge break of trust in the group. When the 'helper' talked about it, he maintained this had been the right thing to do; he claimed he had in effect been following his deepest voice.

"Were you aware of the possible consequences of your action?" I asked. "No," he replied. "Her response came as a total shock!" "In that case, it was not your deepest voice," I said.

Following our deepest voice does not mean blindly following a strong impulse. Our deepest voice comes with an awareness of context.

If we are going to hurt someone through following our deepest voice, we will know that beforehand and prepare ourselves and proceed with deep compassion.

Deepest voice only becomes safe after extensive inner work on ourselves. The man in question had not even begun to sort through the possible blind spots in his 'altruism' – a pattern he freely admitted to having possessed throughout his life. Anyone at any time can identify and a follow a 'deepest voice', but if the inner work on self hasn't been done, if the subject hasn't been uncluttered, it is a gamble as to whether the deepest voice will have any depth at all.

I have no doubt that Saddam Hussein thought he was following his deepest voice when he invaded Kuwait, but it is painfully clear when one reads about him that he had absolutely no experience in disentangling the various voices inside his head. A decision coming from a place of paranoia or greed will never be issued by our deepest voice and at some point is likely to go horribly wrong.

Of course, even after inner work has been done and we have greater discernment as regards our different voices, there is no guarantee. (What's new?) If I have doubts when it comes to the big decisions in life, I do what I call an 'ecology check' with a friend or coach: is there anything I am not seeing? How does my story come over? What might be my blind spots?

Even then, this other person will not become my guide. What he or she says must resonate with something in me. There must be an 'a-ha' inside me, a recognizable movement within my inner world.

So how do you know if you have identified your deepest voice?

All these expressions – 'resonate', 'movement inside', 'a-ha', – aren't they impossibly woolly and dangerously subjective? Isn't it much easier and safer to do as Kant did and create a general principle that everyone can follow: Act only in such a way that can become a universal law for others.

The problem with such moral imperatives is that their only source of guidance is reason. The opposite of reason is not passion, as is so often depicted; neither is it some blind, hysterical impulse. The (complementary) opposite of reason is simply a different kind of knowing, a different kind of felt reality.

The best metaphor I can find is one of tuning an instrument.

Someone who knows and understands musical instruments simply knows when the instrument is out of tune. When they hear a false note there is a kind of inner sensory dissonance.

When my friend told me to keep my heart open to my step-children, there was an initial dissonance in me. Later, though, this turned into a consonance that spread like a warm fluid through my body, as I began to sort through the different voices. Something inside me felt liberated! Even though I was appalled at the prospect of making myself vulnerable again, a weight was off my shoulders. My whole inner energetic system relaxed.

My experience of the deepest voice is that it is rarely a crystal-clear clarion. If only life were so simple! It is more a deeper tone, a different vibration. When I hear that voice, I may still be nervous about going ahead, but there will be some kind of coming to rest in my body, a clearing within my inner world. It will be as if this insight has dropped into the troubled waters of my mind, dispelling much of the murky, oily doubts.

I also know only too well the feeling of not following my deepest voice.

The feeling of tension at telling a lie.

The feeling of contraction and smallness at not daring to make a change I know needs to be made.

The feeling of shame at not standing up for what I think is right.

Postmodern Pete of course will not accept the notion of a deepest voice, because for him everything exists in a relative flatland. No one voice is any deeper or more meaningful than another.

To irk Postmodern Pete even further, I offer a hypothesis that, if I am not careful, might even resemble a meta-narrative: our deepest voice is connected not only to our pleasure impulse, but somehow aligns with the universe around us. That is the point of Goethe's quote at the beginning of this chapter.

Like him, I am suggesting that our deepest voice brings us sooner or later into a kind of flow, in which the traffic lights in our life are more likely to be green than red. This is not a rule of thumb – it is a mysterious principle whose validity you must check against your own experience and judge only in terms of the depth of pleasure gained.

I believe my deepest voice is in some way connected to a deeper current in my life. And that current is essentially benevolent and will bring me to greater pleasures.

See what works for you.

At the end of the day I am a pragmatist with utilitarian leanings.

And my business is pleasure.

Pleasure as a Moving Target

"Did you ever say yes to a pleasure?
Oh my friends, then you also said yes to all pain.
All things are linked, entwined, in love with one another.
"What does not kill me, makes me stronger.""
– Nietzsche

I remember the frantic attempts by my fellow students to find jobs in our last year at university: everyone filling out hundreds of job applications and waiting anxiously for replies. I wasn't remotely interested. I knew what I wanted to do: travel the world. The type of work didn't matter as long as it financed my travels. I would do pretty much anything… and did.

Ten rich, challenging years later, after wandering round the world from job to job, and from country to country, I began to think about work in a different light. I needed work that was meaningful, fulfilling. Up till then, fulfilment had come from the travel, the learning, the adventure. Work had been just a means to an end and I was content with that.

Gradually though, I felt my soul seeking something else, another kind of mission. I started my 'career' from nothing. Now, 15 years later, work is one of my deepest pleasures and it keeps expanding, growing, and inspiring. My mission has slowly taken shape and the present evolution of that mission is this book.

My soul thrives on this: *I love what I do, I do what I love.*

I expect most people can identify a series of different life phases: fulfilling different needs at different ages resulting in different kinds of pleasure.

These changes are motivated primarily by an evolving pleasure impulse.

Pleasure is a moving target.

Deepest voice is the guidance system.

Hedonism means stepping into the unknown of our emerging needs. People often associate hedonism with habitual patterns of behaviour, even addiction. Hedonism as I see it involves a discipline that challenges every habit we have: "Does this still really make me happy?" is the key question.

My hypothesis is that our soul will always seek new pleasure, differing in depth or breadth, or both. Habit is the obstacle. We like to stay in our 'comfort zone'. Of course the comfort zone is named as such for a reason and offers some kind of solace: the solace of avoiding the fear of change.

One part of us does indeed seek homeostasis, rest.

If we attend carefully to the pleasure impulse, it will not lead us to a restless, endless search for new pleasures. Sometimes our greatest pleasure will come from simply enjoying and refining what we have.

For years, I participated in countless workshops and trainings, lived in ashrams and communities, and devoured every possible teaching that was on offer. Now I hardly ever put myself in such contexts.

What gives me most pleasure now is to refine and integrate all I have learnt.

Too much didactic input doesn't help me any more.

Doing nothing new is a new experience for me. And all that may change again... pleasure is a moving target.

There is a natural rhythm of change and coming to settle with that change, a rhythm that is supported by a closely monitored pleasure impulse.

When that alignment process to the change has completed itself, at a certain point the pleasure impulse will change its tune and try to rouse us into some kind of new movement. Part of us will feel dissatisfied, part of us will seek something new. The old pleasures will not be so pleasurable. Another voice in us, however, may simply want to stay in the comfort zone and habit will gradually take over.

The comfort zone is partly created by us, partly by our environment. If we pay close attention to our pleasure impulse we will need at times to challenge both our own patterns and those of the milieu to which we have conformed. *Is this pattern still serving me?*

After a while the comfort zone lulls us into a kind of automatic pilot.

Automatic pilot can function just as much in the ashram as in a bank.

Yet the expression 'comfort zone' is deceptive.

If we look a little deeper, the comfort zone is rarely comfortable.

If we are in some way stuck in habit, there will always be an itch.

An itch that can get worse and worse...

Staying for long in the comfort zone requires denial.

We have to pretend the itch is not there, explain it away, or simply resign ourselves to it. And at that moment of resignation, our capacity for pleasure and joy is diminished.

The deeper pleasures require an openness to change and to learning.

We have to evolve in order to gain maximum pleasure from life.

On the one hand, our sources of pleasure change simply with the aging process – the path from candy to cigars – but if we wish, there is a deeper strand of development that involves a deeper evolution of self.

If we want the deeper pleasures in our life, we have to be able to tear up the book of rules and habit we have swallowed, including the rules we have created for ourselves.

Even within our organic physical and emotional development, the tendency is to find something we like and stick to it. Because something has given us pleasure before, we assume it always will. What in fact often happens is that the original direct pleasure is subsumed into the indirect pleasure of a habit: security and a comfort zone that is not especially comfortable.

But the true hedonist longs for newer, deeper pleasure.

In my wilder flights of philosophical fancy, I would say that the pleasure impulse is one way in which evolution works through us. My belief is that personal and societal evolution are absolutely linked to the pleasure impulse. At the very least, I know the two are connected in my life. My need for new and different kinds of pleasure has forced me to evolve and develop as a person, and in the case of spirit pleasures even beyond personhood.

Just as pleasure is a moving target, so is the subject of pleasure, the self, also forced into motion. Many of the newer, deeper, pleasures can only be enjoyed by a different or expanded self.

A committed hedonist is committed to the transformative act of growing his or her own soul: the experience of growing as a person, the experience of becoming freer from our ego, the experience of liberation from fear, the experience of finding new facets of love. For the committed hedonist, learning becomes a practice, inner empiricism becomes a way of being.

Commitment is needed because learning isn't always fun. Yes, there is the satisfaction of curiosity, the wonder of it all, the excitement of the new, but there is also the terror of the new. Just as the infant encounters exhilaration and dejection in their first faltering steps, the adult encounters the panic and disorientation of the edge of the unknown, along with the joy of liberation and novelty.

The soul world has an edge of sweat and grit and needs courage. We need to be able to go to the scary places in ourselves, confront our demons, poke around in our shadow.

If you don't believe me, have a long, deep conversation with your partner about sex. How much pleasure is there really? Do you really get what you need and want? Are you prepared to confront the ghosts of vulnerability in that particular closet? That is the best chance you have of moving to a deeper level of pleasure in sex. It is tough learning.

There is *always* another level. Pleasure is a moving target. The kind of sex that fulfils you in one phase of your life may not be the same as that which fulfils you in another phase. Put another way: the you of today may not like the same sex as the you of yesterday.

Let us look at pleasure and evolution within the main context of my work: organisations. The workplace has huge potential for learning and fulfilment. Soul pleasure revolves around meaning, the feeling of living from one's deepest values. A sole bottom line of profit or product in an organization, for example, makes no sense if we are talking about the deeper forms of pleasure. For soul pleasure, people need to matter, integrity needs to matter, community needs to matter, loyalty needs to matter, contribution to society needs to matter.

A commercial organization that explicitly places profit above all else might well make a profit in the short term, but will not make anyone happy in any profound way. Purely profit-driven companies are by definition not pleasure-driven, because profit alone will never bring the deepest pleasure. Money alone doesn't make anyone happy unless they are in survival mode – and even then the money gives most satisfaction when it is used to feed one's family or fulfil some other noble goal.

Which will give more of a sense of fulfilment: receiving a return of interest from an organization for which we have no affection or personal connection whatsoever, or receiving a return of interest from a company whose mission and ethos we believe in? There are different levels of pleasure even in the financial world.

The world of finance is impoverished when it comes to pleasure!

People think because big figures are involved and everyone wears suits that there is meaning in it.

Making huge amounts of money, scoring points, does not necessarily have anything to do with a genuine sense of achievement, and the pleasure levels will match accordingly.

Why do people like Bill Gates and Warren Buffett give away billions?

Not just because they can – there are plenty like them who don't – but because they are searching for meaning, or in my language a different kind of pleasure. Andre Agassi says that setting up a school has given him more satisfaction than any of the tennis majors he has won.

Pleasure is a moving target.

That motion is connected to evolution, both internal and external.

The happiest organizations are those that are committed to learning.

Initially, the learning process tends to be focused on technical aspects: productivity, sales, marketing and so on. As an organization grows and matures, if given the space, the learning will expand to include other dimensions. The positive emerging trend in commercial organizations these days is 'triple bottom line': people, planet, profit. The reason for this learning and development is not just greater productivity. The evolution itself brings new kinds of meaning and pleasure to working life.

In order for people and planet to be included in the picture, the interior of the organization has to change. By this, I don't mean the furniture, though that may follow. I am referring to the organization's culture, the shared values and practices of the workers. For the culture or interior of an organization to change, the interior of its people has to change too. They have to grow and develop *as people*, not just as performers.

That is my job: to help facilitate that interior change process.

I am what is sometimes grandly called *a change agent*.

If the people in an organization commit themselves to such a change process, new levels of meaning and fulfilment will be added to their lives. The organization will also function better, but for it to really work, performance and results cannot be the only motivation for change.

This kind of conscious evolutionary process in organizations, however, is no different to any other inner growth process. Sweat, tears and courage are needed, along with the ability to become vulnerable, the ability to admit weakness and fear, the ability to face uncomfortable truths. My work in organizations is really about one thing: helping people out of their egos and into their souls. Such a movement from ego to soul is traditionally seen as a moral issue, but to me it is ultimately a question of pleasure: pleasure for the soul of the individuals and pleasure for the soul of the organization in terms of sustainability and fulfilling its purpose.

We need a fourth 'p': pleasure.

People, planet, profit, pleasure.

As with individuals, the pleasure impulse of an organization can be used to fuel positive change. If workers are not generally happy (enough), that is a sign that change is needed; there is something to learn.

The pleasure impulse, when attended to in the correct, disciplined way, is the rope that will haul us out of the swamp of unnecessary suffering. The job of the pleasure impulse, or rather its gift, is to bring us pleasure. But if we are to enjoy the fruits of the pleasure impulse, either as individuals or as organizations, we must be able to challenge ourselves and look unflinchingly at those areas of our lives in which we are genuinely unhappy or without pleasure. With a firm, loving and compassionate hand, we must coax ourselves and our organizations into a happier life.

The link between pleasure and learning starts, as with all pleasures, in infancy: reaching out, exploring, touching, licking, hitting, strutting, staggering, falling. This is the basic impulse to learn, grow and evolve.

As they grow older, children are often exposed within conventional educational systems to increasingly limited forms of learning that are mostly oriented around the gathering and memorizing of information. Then, after school and university, all serious education stops. Developmental psychologists such as Robert Kegan and Carol Gilligan contend that whole new dimensions of learning and development can keep unfolding all through our lives if given the necessary attention.

The universe appears to gyrate to some vital force of evolution of which we are a part. When it is consciously cherished and nurtured within ourselves, that vital force is experienced as a joy, an intense feeling of being alive. Learning wakes us up. Learning brings meaning and fulfilment to our lives. If you want your soul to die early and give way to a hunched, bitter dotage, a simple course is available to you: stop learning. Stop thinking there are new doors to be opened. Assume you have seen it all. Run your life as if pleasure is no longer a moving target.

A key joy connected to learning is that of liberation. Just as learning to walk liberates the infant from a floor-centered life, the major steps of inner transformation later in life liberate us from the confines of our old world and open up new worlds. While infants learn to stand, we as adults can learn to stand up for ourselves. We can learn to express difficult emotions, we can learn to be honest, we can learn to own our needs, we can learn to be vulnerable and accept support. All these conventional therapeutic or self-developmental goals give deep pleasure as we are released from the shackles of our entrenched patterns and worldviews.

For the person who doesn't know how to hug or be touched, or has forgotten, the sweet pain, release and exhilaration of that new hug can be overwhelming and infectious.

The soul needs to feel fulfilled in order to feel pleasure.
Soul needs to have an activity that involves the whole of us.
Whether that is work, parenting, or studying, devotion is needed.

In work and relationship, we need to keep seeking till we find what grabs our whole being. If we want to feed our soul and derive the consequent pleasure, we need to take risks – give up the safe job that doesn't fulfil us, challenge the relationship we have grown stale in, be open to relocating, to the unknown. Open to change.

Pleasure is a moving target, and a genuine pursuit of that moving target commits us to life-long learning. Learning is both means and goal: learning both increases our capacity for pleasure and gives pleasure in itself.

Because pleasure is linked to evolution and learning, there are pleasures waiting for us on the evolutionary trail beyond our wildest imagination...

Pleasure Metrics

Go for a walk.

Imagine you are in a helicopter looking down.

Take a good look at yourself winding, wending, wandering through life.

Take in all the different strands of your life: work, family, house, love, sex, friends.

Look at the expression on your face, your way of walking along these different paths.

Where are you happy? Where not?

Where does it feel heavy, where does it feel light?

Where is there flow, where does it feel blocked or incomplete?

Where is there chronic pain?

Dare to be objective in your observations of yourself, the subject.

This is the pleasure barometer: the big picture.

We saw in the last chapter how pleasure is a moving target that requires learning. In this chapter we look at the signals that tell us some kind of movement or learning is needed. I have given various examples from my own life of times when I felt a clear change of wind, perceived in part intuitively, in part through some kind of dissatisfaction in my life.

One reason we are not always alert to our pleasure barometer is because we are so busy trying to do the right thing, regardless of how much pleasure we experience as a result of this 'right thing'. Two practices are needed to extricate ourselves from the world of truths-and-norms that can so deaden our sensitivity to the pleasure barometer.

The first practice is *inner empiricism*: look inside and observe.

The second practice is a particular kind of *psychological emancipation*: we have to give ourselves permission to be happy. This may sound to some like an injunction from the cheesiest self-help book, or a ghastly invitation to a new-age ball. But the fact is, without really opening our minds and hearts to the possibility of deep fulfilment, we will remain stuck in old, pleasureless patterns.

These patterns run deep.

Apart from our individual psychological history, we are loyal to the misery of those who have gone before us.

Our pasts are riddled with trauma and tragedy. Everybody's past.

Unconsciously, we follow in the sad footsteps of our forebears and feel guilty if we are happier than them.

Unconsciously, we will hold on to the familial and cultural norms that surround us. We act either in blind obedience or blind rebellion to these norms, rather than carve out our own path to pleasure. It is as if we have to betray somebody or something in order to be happy.

Unhooking ourselves from our individual and collective past is often the first step on the road to pleasure. We neither can nor need to be totally free from our past, but the unconscious manacles must at least be loosened. Then we begin to grow a soul that can breathe, take in the new, and contemplate a life of deeper pleasure.

THE DISCIPLINE OF PLEASURE

Inner empiricism brings us back to the here-and-now of our bodies and away from convention and automatic pilot. Then we can begin to pay homage at the temple of pleasure.

Through developing inner empiricism we learn to receive and value data from our own monitor, rather than relying on external data in the form of truth-and-norms. We become our own reference point, rather than relying on the reference point of the systems to which we belong. If we only follow external sources, do our duty, do 'the right thing', our inner feelings won't really matter. The pleasure impulse is fulfilled (in meagre fashion) by following norms and feeling secure through that convention. For the true hedonist our inner feelings absolutely matter, but first the whole registering process within our inner world needs to be refined and sharpened.

The pleasure barometer monitors the big picture of our lives: the chronic, long-term threads of relationship, family, work, community, location and so on. Through taking the helicopter position described at the beginning of the chapter, we can monitor the macro-level pleasure of our lives, where words such as happiness and fulfilment tend to be used.

The sensing mechanism for the micro-level is more like a thermometer than a barometer – more short term, more acute, more accurate.

Here is a sentence that shows the pleasure thermometer at work:

"That conversation left me with a sour taste in my mouth."

How de we know something was "off" with that conversation?

Because of the "sour taste left in the mouth". Figurative or not, this is the exact kind of data from our inner landscape that provides guidance. Through this feeling of displeasure, we know that we have not been authentic, for example, or have been manipulated.

The only way we can redress that discomfort is by returning to the conversation and saying what we didn't say or by coming to a deeper level of acceptance of some problematic issue. Then we return to a state of ease and comfort within ourselves. Or, in another language, our soul is back in charge not our ego.

If we come away from an encounter feeling bad, or as a 'perpetrator' – through saying too much, for example, or saying it too violently – then the bad feeling in our stomachs, or wherever it is situated in our body, will only be alleviated by saying sorry or some other kind of rapprochement.

When we come away from an encounter moist with the dew of pleasure, it is worth paying heed to what has just happened and with whom. This is likely to be an indicator of a positive direction, one that needs more attention in our lives.

This is how the pleasure thermometer works on a micro-level: using our inner monitor, we simply gauge our levels of pleasure and pain and act accordingly.

This is hardly news. Pleasure and pain are an obvious part of our world. That's why they offer such a practical measurement tool. But do we use this tool properly? Are we consistent and thorough enough in using it?

Needless to say, because of the intensely subjective nature of our inner monitor, because we thereby abandon the safety net of external truth-and-norms as guides for our behaviour, we do need some kind of external reference point.

We need intimates. We need people with whom we can share our inner world in an intimate way. This can be a friend, a colleague, a coach or counsellor. We need people in our lives that can add some kind of corroboration or inter-subjectivity to our self-analyses. But these people need to be able to put aside their own book of truths and regard us from an empty mind and with a full heart.

Intimates are those we can trust.

Trust means we can rely on both their honesty and support.

Friends who can't say the hard things to us are not real friends. Friends who don't wish from the bottom of their hearts for us to be happy are not real friends.

The problem is that we cannot always see on our own what makes us happy. We deceive ourselves; we mistake ego pleasure for the deeper pleasures and thereby deprive ourselves.

Ego is based on fear and control and derives its pleasure from avoiding the former and exerting the latter. Soul seeks health and well-being for all.

We need other people to help us in the pleasure endeavour. This mitigates the subjectivity, but leaves us in the driving seat.

The Pleasure Compass

"Ask yourself whether you are happy and you cease to be so."
– John Stuart Mill

The pleasure meters are a vital part of the quest for pleasure. By developing and sharpening these meters, we can ensure that we are on the right path. On the level of soul, if a course we have chosen in our life brings consistent unhappiness, we need to confront that reality and change course appropriately. If there is insufficient simple pleasure in our lives and we fail to enjoy the little things, there is inner work to be done. You can be as busy as a bee but you still need to check how much honey results.

How utterly obvious!

Funny how often we fail to make these assessments.

Pleasure is not only the measuring stick but also the goal itself. Thanks to the pleasure paradox, pleasure as goal is a tricky business. Various thinkers such as John Stuart Mill above have concluded that pleasure is a purely concomitant phenomenon, a by-product that slips in via the backdoor as we are absorbed in something else and should not be targeted as such. The more you want, the less you get. Or put another way, too much desire gets in the way.

This is especially true for the deeper pleasures of soul and spirit, which require a more subtle seduction to yield their fruits than a head-on charge for pleasure.

On the other hand, what I have found is that if pleasure falls off the radar, this does not help either. As with any kind of goal, we need the energy and focus of intention to help us realize our longings.

Pleasure does indeed need to remain the ultimate goal, the North star in our lives. Subconsciously, the pleasure impulse is so strong that this is happening anyway, albeit in a primitive way, but as I have explained the impulse needs to be refined and aligned with our conscious intent.

If we forget that pleasure is the ultimate goal, we are likely to fall (again) into truth-and-norms thought and action, where doing one's duty takes over.

We need a pleasure compass because we need both directionality and a means of checking whether that direction is being maintained. The image of the compass is also appropriate because a compass doesn't actually tell you *how* to get where you want.

The fact that pleasure is a moving target plus the effect of the pleasure paradox ensure the route to pleasure is rarely straight. To go where Coleridge went in Xanadu, to arrive at the greatest pleasure domes, we often have to give up on a two-dimensional map and linear route. If we want to feast on honey and drink the milk of paradise, discipline, creativity and a taste for the unknown are needed. We may even have to enter deep romantic chasms and savage places to get there.

Drugs are an exception in that they do generally provide instant pleasure, but that pleasure can easily turn into suffering as countless examples demonstrate. Furthermore drugs cannot provide pleasure that is sustainable. They provide simple pleasure that can slip into spirit pleasure, but the effect is short-term and a sharp pleasure dip is often experienced afterwards. Ego pleasures are also more readily available, but as we have already seen, the pleasure is superficial and sooner or later results in pain.

On a two-dimensional map, there is always a quickest or shortest route. These days we just switch on the satellite system in the car or on the iPhone. The hedonist, however, has no standard map. She is on her own, surrounded by others on their own.

Just you and I, finding out as we go along, giving each other a few tips on the way.

Your particular path to pleasure will be different to mine. Trying to create and follow a standardized route (if this was possible) would only lead us back into a truth-and-norms rut.

When I was 23, I went to live in a spiritual community in Switzerland centred round a charismatic teacher, Michael Barnett, who became a lifelong mentor and friend. I was there for just over a year and most of the time it was hell. I felt overwhelmed, turned upside down, utterly vulnerable, utterly inadequate. Yet I felt exactly in the right place at the right time. I felt movement, I felt my soul growing. If the pleasure map was two-dimensional, the shortest route would have been to avoid the pain and leave the community, but a multi-dimensional map does not always disclose routes that are direct or obvious. Those two years of 'hell' laid a foundation for heaven.

Freud points to something similar in his theory of deferred gratification, but I think it goes even deeper: the soul (a concept probably abhorrent to Freud) knows of the greater pleasure domes available and is connected to a deeper stream of meaning and pleasure possible to life.

The pleasure/pain apparatus we receive as a biological given is primitive, part of Freud's id. The apparatus has to be worked and developed, but it is a constant. What we can bring is discipline: an attitude of discovery and learning.

Simple pleasures demand a heart of awareness, soul pleasures demand courage and commitment, spirit pleasures demand the dissolution of our identity. All the deeper pleasures demand an inner maturity, a relaxation of the ego's grip on our lives. If we make ourselves too big or too small, we pay the price in pleasure.

Love and Lovelessness

I feel dry on the inside.
Not the clean healthy dry soul of Heraclitus.
More cracked-earth-dry, no water, no lubricant, no energy.
I feel empty.
Not the brimming emptiness of a Zen master.
I don't feel at home in myself, I don't feel connected to my surroundings.
I feel lifeless, loveless. I feel alone and lonely.
Everything feels hollow – relationship, work, hobbies, and even sex.
Imagine having an orgasm with no pleasure.
Imagine a mango without sweetness.

Technically, this state of pleasurelessness is called *anhedonia*… a grand-sounding word that might lend a brief sense of dignity to this wretched state.

Who has not experienced this pleasure void at some point(s) in their lives?

Anhedonia is usually associated with specific mental disorders and neurological problems, but, like most symptoms of mental disorder, pleasurelessness is familiar to all of us, even if only in a milder form.

Anhedonia is not the same as pain. Pain can easily turn into pleasure, through release. There is no release from anhedonia because there is no tension. It is a deadness, an absence, which is in some ways harder to deal with than pain.

So what exactly is dead?

I speculate, based on my own experience, that this state of anhedonia is more fundamental than some specific lack in our lives – of love, of success, of a happy family. I mentioned earlier how my son often seems to vibrate in a joyful way, regardless of what he is doing. Feeling alive in an alive body is essentially pleasurable. I also know that feeling, as if there is some *élan vital* or Qi, some invisible force in the universe that energizes us. Our basic *joie de vivre* seems connected to this force.

Anhedonia describes the state of not feeling this life force. We are therefore alive and not alive. Our body goes through the motions. On the most fundamental level, life is not enjoyable to us.

And that is intolerable.

Of course neuroscience explains anhedonia in very different terms. It is very likely there will be some correlating brain dysfunction, but, as with all purely physiological explanations for psychological states, we are left feeling even more lonely in our subjective experiential world. We need explanations and solutions that also engage our subjective world.

The good news is that such a state is prescient of some kind of change wanting to happen. Such a state is an opportunity to find different sources and deeper levels of pleasure. The usual kicks don't give a kick, the usual pleasure channels have dried up. When I really go into the feeling, rather than try and change it, there is usually a hidden jewel waiting to be revealed. When I stop fighting the experience, accept the loss, my inner landscape begins slowly to change and the desert discloses other possibilities. Anhedonia

THE DISCIPLINE OF PLEASURE

is a sign that North on the pleasure compass has shifted; the soul has to get to work.

If you can't accept the pleasurelessness and it doesn't go away over time, you might find yourself wondering: what is the point in living?

Imagine life without pleasure of any kind.

Would you sign up for that?

People who take their own lives are often judged harshly.

Consider first what a life devoid of pleasure would feel like.

Pleasure is a serious issue.

Pleasure is what makes life worthwhile.

Love and Pleasure

Pleasure was born from the union between Cupid and Psyche.
The place where love and soul meet.

According to Keats, love lies at the apex of the 'pleasure thermometer'.

Psychologist Alexander Lowen suggests in his book *Pleasure* that we simply love that which gives us pleasure.

Love covers a large gamut of applications: from passion to compassion, from "Romeo, Romeo…" to "I love chocolate mousse" to "Love thy neighbour as thyself". It is hard to imagine any of these experiences of love happening without pleasure. Love is inextricably linked to pleasure.

Presumably love is one of the first pleasures we experience. The initial outpouring of love between parent and child is more or less invincible except in extreme circumstances. That original maternal cuddle turns into the blissful embrace of our beloved in later life – and provides Freudians with a wealth of material to work with. The object of our love may change, the context of our love may change, but does the basic love vibe really change? Does that delicious feeling of… *love* change? Do we ever tire of that feeling?

Is love, as Bertrand Russell said, the only thing of absolute value?

In Western traditions, love is revered by everyone from Plato to St Paul and St Augustine. The Christian religion in particular extols love beyond all other states of being. Perhaps this is not only the case in the West: in his own way, the Dalai Lama does the same. Asked what is at the core of all religions, this tremendously learned Tibetan Buddhist gave an immediate answer which continues to resonate with me 15 years after I heard him say it: "Warm heart!"

All the pleasures I have listed – are they not all connected in some way to love? The simple pleasure of hearing a bird sing… do we not feel some kind of love for that particular expression of life? The soul pleasure of creating a great meal… is the love of the cook not one of the ingredients? The spirit pleasure of melting into the big One… do we not feel universal love in such moments?

Even ego pleasures include an element of love, a perverse form of self-love as we seek to put ourselves above others. There is even an element of love when we put ourselves below others and take the role of victim. Self-pity is a distorted form of love for ourselves.

Various spiritual teachers, including Osho and Eckhart Tolle, have said that love is ultimately a *state of being* rather than an attachment to a particular object. Love wells up from inside and then finds something or somebody to land on. If this is so, what a source of pleasure… it is right there inside our psyche! No drugs are needed, no lovers, no career, no family, no children – just the act of being alive and in touch with our hearts.

Any serious hedonist cannot but look to love.

If love is the flower, all the traditional virtues related to love, such as gratitude, compassion, devotion, are the petals. Unfortunately these qualities, these miraculous gifts, tend to be approached from a truth-and-norms perspective. How many times have we heard the expression, "You should be grateful!"? These qualities are worth aiming for because they feel good in themselves, not because they form part of a deontological code to which we are meant to adhere. Part of that feel-good is of course the communion with others that is involved.

Love and its petals cannot be demanded, cannot be forced, cannot be manipulated. Love in its purest form is a state of being, an effortless consequence of being alive. But we are not born with that state alone. Anyone with any experience of children knows that love is mixed from an early age with anger, hatred, cruelty, and vindictiveness. The breast that is loved easily becomes the breast that is hated; a friend is as easily scorned as cherished. The idea of a *tabula rasa* at birth seems ridiculous to me. Genetically, culturally, systemically, we are born with and into all kinds of psychological baggage that often becomes heavier still through our upbringing.

Opening our hearts, breaking through the ice of all our past hurts, is hard work. Soul work. But the prize of love is worth the struggle, the joy of intimacy is one of the pearls in the pleasure chest. If you are seriously interested in pleasure, you have no choice but to explore the garden of love.

When Cupid and Psyche were joined, the offspring was pleasure.

ABOUT THE AUTHOR

JAMES BAMPFIELD was born in 1964 and grew up in rural England. Intensely curious from an early age, he passed successfully through the academic hoops put before him, culminating in Cambridge University. He soon realized however that the deeper existential questions to which he was drawn were not to be answered merely by the intellect, so after graduating he launched himself on a spiritual odyssey that took him to various countries, gurus, teachers and communities. Jobs on the way varied from restaurant work to teaching at Japanese universities.

In his early thirties he decided he was finally ready to put work first and went back to university to study the science of change in individuals and organizations. Since the formation of the company Quinx in 2002, where he is a founding partner, he has worked as a consultant and facilitator in contexts as various as multinationals and NGO's in the Middle-East.

He is married with one child and three stepchildren and lives in Belgium, though his work often takes him to the US and various other countries.

He is still intensely curious…

INFLUENTIAL BOOKS

Epicurus: *The Essential Epicurus*

Sigmund Freud: *Beyond the Pleasure Principle*

Carol Gilligan: *The Birth of Pleasure*

Dalai Lama: *Happiness*

David J. Linden: *The Pleasure Compass*

Alexander Lowen: *Pleasure*

Michel Foucault: *The Use of Pleasure*

Osho: *The Way of the White Clouds*

Michael Barnett: *Hints on the Art of Jumping*

Ken Wilber: *Sex, Ecology and Spirituality*

Diane Eisler: *Sacred Pleasure*

The Romantic Poets